How to really love your child

D. Ross Campbell, M.D.

While this book is designed for the reader's personal profit and enjoyment, it is also intended for group study. A Leader's Guide with Victor Multiuse Transparency Masters is available from your local bookstore or from the publisher.

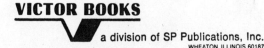
VICTOR BOOKS

a division of SP Publications, Inc.
WHEATON. ILLINOIS 60187

Offices also in Fullerton. California • Whitby. Ontario. Canada • Amersham-on-the-Hill, Bucks, England

Unless otherwise noted, Scripture quotations are from the King James Version (KJV); the *New American Standard Bible* (NASB) © The Lockman Foundation, 1960, 1962, 1963, 1968, 1971, 1972, 1973; *The Living Bible* (LB), © 1971 Tyndale House Publishers; the *New International Version* (NIV) © 1978 by the New York International Bible Society. All quotations used by permission.

Dewey Decimal Classification: 155.4
  Suggested Subject Heading: CHILD STUDY

Library of Congress Catalog Card Number: 77-89470
ISBN: 0-88207-816-x

First printed in paperback 1977

VICTOR BOOKS
A division of SP Publications, Inc.
P.O. Box 1825 • Wheaton, Illinois 60187

Contents

Foreword

This book hits us where we live. Yet it does not condemn—but tells us how to be parents in a different and constructive fashion. It is compassionate without being permissive.

Parents have never been trained to be parents. They tend to rear a child without any real fixed standards. Even the successes seem to be primarily by accident; this book is designed to produce successes by intention.

Dr. Ross Campbell has something vitally valuable to say—and says it plainly so we can understand it. This psychiatrist establishes himself in this book as a man of deep personal insight, deep spiritual values, and a great sensitivity both to the children and their parents. He doesn't hesitate to share himself and his own family experiences in illustrating what he has to say.

This is a book you will want to *read* and *reread*. It's that loaded with practical, usable information! Both your mind and your heart will tell you this book is true.

Ben Haden
Speaker, "Changed Lives,"
Chattanooga, Tennessee

Preface

This is a book written primarily for parents of children younger than adolescents. Its intention is to give mothers and fathers an understandable and usable way of approaching their wonderful, yet awesome, task of raising each child.

I have tried to present my message to parents in the clearest, most basic way I know. My concerns are the needs of a child and how best to meet them.

This whole area of child raising is in itself a complex venture with which most parents today are having great difficulty. Unfortunately, the outpouring of books, articles, lectures, and seminars regarding children have largely frustrated and bewildered parents rather than helped them. This is sad because most of these sources of information have been excellent.

I believe the problem has been that many books, articles, and lectures have homed in on one, or at most, only a few very specific aspects of child rearing without covering the subject fully, or without defining the specific area they are covering. Consequently, many conscientious parents have earnestly attempted to apply what they have read or heard as the fundamental way of relating to a child, and this often fails. This failure is not usually due to error in the information read or heard, nor in the way it is applied.

I have found the source of the problem usually lies in the parents not having a general, balanced perspective on how to relate to a child. Most parents have the essential information per se, but there is confusion about *when* to apply *which* principle under *what* circumstance. This confusion is understandable. Many have told parents what to do, but not when to do it nor, in many cases, how to do it.

The classic example of this is in the area of discipline. Excellent books and seminars on childhood have addressed the issue of discipline, but failed to make clear that discipline is only one way of relating to a child. Many parents consequently conclude that discipline is the basic and primary way of treating a child. This is an easy mistake to make especially when one hears the statement, "If you love your child, you must discipline your child." This statement is of course true, but the tragedy is that many parents discipline almost *totally* while showing little love which can be felt or bring comfort to the child. Hence, most children doubt that they are genuinely, unconditionally loved. So, again, the problem is not whether to discipline; the problem is how to manifest our love to a child through discipline and when to show it in other, more affectionate, ways.

I hope to address these problems in a quite plain understandable way, in order to demonstrate how to *generally* approach child raising. In addition, I hope to provide information which will help parents to determine the correct action for each situation. Of course handling every circumstance correctly is impossible; however, the closer we come to this, the better parents we become, the more gratified we are, and the happier our child becomes.

Much of the material in this book has come from lecture series given over the last three years at numerous conferences on parent-child relationships.

1

The Problem

"He was such a good boy, so well behaved," the grieving parents began as they unfolded their painful story in my counseling room. "Yes, he seemed content and never gave us much trouble. We made sure he had the right experiences—scouts, baseball, church and all. He's forever fighting with his brother and sister—but that's just sibling rivalry, isn't it? Other than that, Tom's never been a real problem for us. He is moody sometimes and goes to his room for long periods. But he has never been disrespectful or disobeyed or back-talked. His father saw to that. There's one thing we *know* he has gotten plenty of and that's discipline. In fact, that's the most puzzling thing of all. How can a child so well disciplined all his life suddenly run around with undisciplined peers and do the things they do? And treat adults and parents that way. They even lie, steal, and drink alcohol. I can't trust him. I can't talk to him and he won't talk to me. He's so sullen and quiet. He won't even look at me. He doesn't seem to want anything to do with us. And he's doing so poorly in school this year."

"When did you notice these changes in Tom?" I asked.

"Let's see," replied Mrs. Smith, "he's 14 now. His grades were the first problems we noticed. About two years ago. During the last few months of the sixth grade we noticed he became bored first with school, then with other things. He began to hate going to church. Later Tom even lost interest in his friends and spent more and more time by himself, usually in his room. He talked less and less.

"But things really worsened when he began junior high school. Tom lost interest in his favorite activities—even sports. That's when he completely dropped his old standby friends and began running around with boys who were usually in trouble. Tom's attitude changed and conformed to theirs. He placed little value in grades and wouldn't study. These friends of his often got him in trouble.

"And we've tried everything," Mrs. Smith continued. "First we spanked him. Then we took away privileges like television, movies, and so on. One time we grounded him a solid month. We've tried to reward him for appropriate behavior. I really believe we have tried every recommendation we have heard or read. I really wonder if anyone can help us or help Tom.

"What did we do wrong? Are we bad parents? God knows we've tried hard enough. Maybe it's congenital. Maybe it's something Tom inherited. Could it be physical? But our pediatrician examined him a couple of weeks ago. Should we take him to a gland specialist? Should we get an EEG? We need help. Tom needs help. We love our boy, Dr. Campbell. What can we do to help him? Something's got to be done."

Later, after Mr. and Mrs. Smith departed, Tom entered the counseling room. I was impressed with his naturally likable ways and handsome appearance. His gaze was downcast and when he would make eye contact, it was only for a moment. Although obviously a bright lad, Tom spoke only in short, gruff phrases and grunts. However, when Tom felt comfortable enough to share his story, he revealed essentially the same factual material as his parents. Going further, he said, "No one really cares about me except my friends."

"No one?" I asked.

"Naw. Maybe my parents. I don't know. I used to think they cared about me when I was little. I guess it doesn't matter much now anyway. All they really care about is their own friends, jobs, activities, and things.

"They don't need to know what I do, anyway. It's none of their business. I just want to be away from them and lead my own life. Why should they be so concerned about me? They never were before."

As the conversation progressed, it became clear that Tom was quite depressed, never having times when he felt content with himself or his life. Tom had longed for a close, warm relationship with his parents as long as he could remember, but during the last few months he had slowly given up his dream. He turned to peers who would accept him, but his unhappiness deepened even more.

So here is a common but tragic situation today. An early-adolescent boy who, by all apparent indications, was doing well during his early years. Until he was around 12 or 13 years old, no one guessed that Tom was unhappy. During those years he was a complacent child who made few demands on his parents, teachers, or others. So none suspected that Tom did not feel completely loved and accepted. Despite his having parents who deeply loved him and cared for him, Tom did not *feel* genuinely loved. Yes, Tom knew of his parents' love and concern for him and never would have told you otherwise. Nonetheless, the incomparable emotional well-being of feeling completely and unconditionally loved and accepted was not Tom's.

This is truly difficult to understand, because Tom's parents are indeed good parents. They love him, and take care of his needs to the best of their knowledge. In raising Tom Mr. and Mrs. Smith have applied what they have heard and read, and have sought advice from others. And their marriage is definitely above average. They do love and respect each other.

A Familiar Story

Most parents are having a difficult time raising their child. With pressures and strains mounting every day upon the American family, it is easy to become confused and discouraged. Rising divorce rates, economic crises, declining quality of education, and loss of trust in leadership all take an emotional toll of everyone. As parents become more physically, emotionally, and spiritually drained, it becomes increasingly difficult to nurture their child. I am convinced that a child takes the greatest brunt of these difficult times. A child is the most needy person in our society, and his greatest need is love.

The story of Tom is familiar today. Tom's parents do love him deeply. They have done their best in raising him, but something is missing. Did you notice what it was? No, not love, the parents *do* love him. The basic problem is that Tom does not *feel* loved. Should the parents be blamed? Is it their fault? I don't think so. The truth is that Mr. and Mrs. Smith have always loved Tom, but never knew how to show it. Like most parents, they have a vague idea of what a child needs: food, shelter, clothes, education, love, guidance, etc. All these needs have been met except love, unconditional love. Although love is within the heart of almost all parents, the challenge is to convey this love to their child.

I believe that, despite the problems in today's living, any parents who genuinely desire to give a child what he needs, can be taught to do so. In order to give him everything they can in the short time he is with them, all parents need to know how to truly love their child.

Which Form of Discipline Is Most Appropriate?

"I remember one time when I was six or seven. Even now it makes me unhappy to think about it, and sometimes it makes me mad," went on Tom a few days later. "I had accidentally broken a window with a baseball. I felt terrible about it and hid in the woods until Mom came looking for me. I was so sorry and I remember crying because I felt I had been very bad. When Dad came home, Mom told him about the window and he whipped me." Tears had welled up in Tom's eyes.

I asked, "What did you say then?"

He choked, "Nothing."

This incident illustrates another area of confusion in handling children, that of discipline. In this example, the way Tom was disciplined caused him to have feelings of pain, anger, and resentment toward his parents which he will never forget or forgive without help.

Seven years afterward, Tom still hurts from that happening. Why does that particular incident make such an unpleasant imprint on Tom's memory? There were other times when Tom accepted spankings with no problems, and on occasion was even thankful. Could it have been because he already felt sorry and repentant over his breaking the window? Had he already suffered enough for his mistake without enduring physical pain? Could the spanking have convinced Tom that his parents did not understand him as a person or were not sensitive to his feelings? Could Tom have needed his parents' warmth and understanding at that particular time rather than harsh punishment? If so, how could Tom's parents know? And, if so, how could they discern which form of discipline was most appropriate at that particular time?

What do you think, fellow parents? Should we decide in advance what action we will routinely take in raising a child? Do you think we should be consistent? How consistent? Should we use punishment each time our child misbehaves? If so, should it always be the same? If not, what are the alternatives? What is discipline? Are discipline and punishment synonymous? Should we study one school of thought, for example, Parent Effectiveness Training, and stick by it? Or should we use some of our own common sense and intuition? Or some of each? How much? When?

These are questions every conscientious parent is struggling with today. We are bombarded with books, articles, seminars, and institutes about how to raise our children. Approaches vary from pinching a child's trapezius muscle to the use of candy as a reward.

In short, how could the parents have handled this situation in a way that would discipline Tom and yet maintain a loving, warm relationship with him? We'll look into this difficult subject later.

I think all parents agree that raising a child today is especially difficult. One reason is that so much of a child's time is under the control and influence of others, for instance, school, church, neighbors, and peers. Because of this many parents feel no matter how good a job they do, their efforts have little overall effect upon their child.

The Opposite Is True

Just the opposite is true. Every study I've read indicates that the home wins hands down in every case. The influence of parents far outweighs everything else. The home holds the upper hand in determining how happy, secure, and stable a child is; how a child gets along with adults, peers, and different children; how confident a youngster is in himself and his abilities; how affectionate he is or how aloof; how he responds to unfamiliar situations. Yes, the home, despite many distractions for a child, has the greatest influence on him.

But the home is not the only thing that determines what a child becomes. We had better not make the mistake of totally blaming the home for every problem or disappointment. For the sake of fairness and completeness, I believe we must take a look at the second greatest influence upon a child.

Congenital Temperament

Actually there are many congenital temperaments. Nine have been identified to date. The research which has given us this knowledge has been done by Stella Chess and Alexander Thomas. The data have been reported in their book, *Temperament and Behavior Disorder in Children.* (New York: Univ. Press, 1968)

This book has been acclaimed a classic and is a truly great contribution to the world of behavioral science. It goes a long way in explaining why children have the individual characteristics they do. It helps explain why some children are easier to raise than others. Why some children are more lovable or easier to handle. Why children raised in the same family or in very similar circumstances can be so different.

Best of all, Drs. Chess and Thomas have shown that how a child turns out is determined not only by the home environment, but also by his own personal traits. This has had wonderful results in alleviating much unjustified blame toward parents of children with problems. It is an unfortunate habit of many (including professionals) to assume that parents are fully to blame for everything regarding their child. The research of Chess and Thomas proves that some children are more prone to difficulties than others.

Let's look briefly at their research. Nine temperaments that can be identified in a newborn nursery have been described. These temperaments are not only congenital (present at birth) but are basic characteristics of a child and tend to stay with him. These characteristics can be modified by a child's environment; nonetheless, the temperaments are well ingrained in a child's total personality, do not change easily, and can persist throughout life. Let's look at these congenital temperaments.

1. *Activity level* is the degree of motor activity a child inherently possesses, and determines how active or passive he is.

2. *Rhythmicity* (regularity versus irregularity) is the predictability of such functions as hunger, feeding pattern, elimination, and sleep-wake cycle.

3. *Approach or withdrawal* is the nature of a child's response to a new stimulus such as a new food, toy, or person.

4. *Adaptability* is the speed and ease with which a current behavior is able to be modified in response to altered environmental structuring.

5. *Intensity of reaction* is the amount of energy used in mood expression.

6. *Threshhold of responsiveness* is the intensity level of stimulus required to make a response.

7. *Quality of mood* (positive mood versus negative mood): playful, pleasant, joyful, friendly, as contrasted with unpleasant, crying, unfriendly behavior.

8. *Distractability* identifies the effect of extraneous environment on direction of ongoing behavior.

9. *Attention span and persistence* is the length of time an activity is pursued by a child and the continuation of an activity in face of obstacles.

As you probably noticed, the third, fourth, fifth, and seventh temperaments are the most crucial in determining whether a child will be easy or difficult to raise and care for. A child with a high degree of reactivity (highly "emotional"); a child who tends to withdraw in a new situation (a "withdrawer"); a child who has difficulty adapting to new situations (cannot tolerate change); or a child who is usually in a bad mood. These children are quite vulnerable to stress, especially to high parental expectations. And unfortunately these children tend to receive less love and affection from adults.

The lesson to learn here is that a child's basic characteristics have much to do with the type of mothering and nurturing he receives.

Using these nine temperaments, Chess and Thomas assigned numerical values to evaluate newborn children. From this data they were able to predict clearly which children would be "easy babies", that is, easy to care for, easy to relate to, and easy to raise. The children who were difficult to care for, difficult to relate to, and difficult to raise were called "difficult babies." They would require more from their mothers than would "easy babies."

Then Chess and Thomas compared how the children progressed according to the type of mothering they received. Chess and Thomas studied the babies with "nurturing" mothers (mothers who wanted their children and were able to provide a loving atmosphere where the children felt accepted). The two researchers also studied "non-nurturing" mothers (mothers who consciously or subconsciously rejected their babies or were not able to provide an atmosphere where the children felt accepted and loved). The graph on page 17 summarizes their findings.

As you can see, the "easy" babies and "nurturing" mothers were a great combination. These children developed well with almost no negative consequences.

The "nurturing" mothers with "difficult" babies had some problems with their children, but these situations were overwhelmingly positive. Overall, in the loving atmosphere provided by their mothers, these children did well.

The "easy" babies who had "non-nurturing" mothers gener

	Nurturing Mothers		Nonnurturing Mothers	
Easy babies	+	+	+	−
Difficult babies	+	−	−	−

ally did not do as well. They had more difficulties than the "difficult" babies with nurturing mothers. Their experiences were somewhat more negative than positive.

As you have probably already anticipated, the "difficult" babies with the the "non-nurturing" mothers were most unfortunate. These poor children were in such difficult predicaments that they were aptly called "high-risk" children. The situation of these children is heartbreaking. They are in danger of everything imaginable from child-abuse to abandonment. They are indeed our high-risk children.

So, as we put all this invaluable material together, some extremely important facts begin to emerge. First of all, how a child gets along in the world does not depend only on his home environment and parenting. The basic congenital characteristics of each child have a strong effect on how he develops, progresses, and matures.

These traits also affect and often determine how easy or difficult a child is to care for and how frustrating he might be to his parents. This, in turn, influences the parents' handling of a child. It's a two-way street.

Learning these facts has helped many guilt-ridden parents in my daily practice.

Another important lesson for parents to learn is that despite what type of congenital temperaments a child may possess, the type of mothering (and fathering, of course) is more important in determining how a child will do. Study the graph again. Although a "difficult" child is of course more difficult to raise, the type of emotional nurturing has more influence in determining the final outcome. Parenting can change these congenital temperaments positively or negatively.

That's what this book is all about. It's a how-to book: how to relate to your child so he will grow to be his best; how to give your child the emotional nurturing he needs so badly. It is impossible to cover every aspect of child rearing here. I have therefore included what I feel is the most basic material for effective parenting.

It is a fact that most parents have a feeling of love toward their children. It is *assumed,* however, that parents naturally convey this love to a child. This is the greatest error today. Most parents are not transmitting their own heartfelt love to their children, and the reason is that they do not know how. Consequently, many children today do not feel genuinely, unconditionally loved and accepted.

This, I feel, is the case in most children's problems today. Unless parents have a basic love-bond relationship with their child, everything else (discipline, peer relationships, school performance) is on a faulty foundation and problems will result.

This book provides the crucial basics in establishing a love-bond relationship.

2

The Setting

Before we get into the meat of how to genuinely love and discipline a child, it is important to look at the prerequisites of good child rearing. The first and most important of these is the home. We will touch only a few of the essential points.

The most important relationship in the family is the marital relationship. It takes primacy over all others including the parent-child relationship. Both the quality of the parent-child bond and the child's security are largely dependent on the quality of the marital bond. So you can see why it is important to assure the best possible relationship between wife and husband before seriously attempting to relate to our child in more positive ways. We can summate that the better our marital relationship, the more effective and gratifying will be the application of later information.

We can start by realizing that there is a difference between cognitive (that is, intellectual or rational) communications and emotional (that is, feeling) communications. Persons who communicate primarily on a cognitive level deal mainly with factual data. They like to talk about such topics as sports, the stock market, money, houses, jobs, etc, keeping the subject of conversation out of the emotional area. Usually they are quite uncom-

fortable dealing with issues which elicit feelings, especially
unpleasant feelings such as anger. Consequently, they avoid talking about subjects which involve love, fear, and anger. These
persons have difficulty, then, being warm and supportive of their
spouses.

Others communicate more on the feeling level. They tire easily
of purely factual data, and feel a need to share feelings, especially
with their spouses. They feel the atmosphere between husband
and wife must be as free as possible from unpleasant feelings like
tension, anger, and resentment. So, of course, they want to talk
about these emotional things, resolve conflicts with their spouse,
clear the air, and keep things pleasant between them.

Of course no one is completely cognitive or completely emotional. We will all be somewhere on the spectrum this simple
graph shows. If a person's personality and communication pat-

Emotional   **Cognitive**

terns tended to be almost completely emotional in *manifestation*
this person would appear on the left side of the graph. If a person
exhibited a cognitive pattern of communication, he/she would
be on the right side of the graph. We all fit somewhere between
the two extremes. Where do you fit in?

Where would you say men and women tend to be on the chart?
Right! As a general rule, women tend to be more emotional in
their ways of dealing with other persons, especially spouse and
child. Men tend to be more cognitive in their ways of communicating.

At this point, I'll bet you are supposing that being on the right
side of the graph is more desirable than appearing on the left.
This is a common misconception today. The truth is that every
type of personality has advantages and disadvantages. A person

on the left side of the graph, who shares more feelings, is not less bright or less intellectual. This person is simply aware of his/her feelings and is usually better able to do something about them. On the other hand, a person on the right side of the graph, who displays less feelings, does not *have* less feelings, the feelings are simply suppressed and buried, and this person is less aware and often blind to his feelings.

A surprising fact is that the so-called cognitive person (on the right) is controlled by his feelings just as is the so-called emotional person but *he doesn't realize it.* For example, the stiff, formal intellectual has deep feelings also, but uses enormous energy to keep them buried so he won't be bothered with them. But unfortunately they *do* bother him. Whenever someone (like an "emotional" wife, or child) is around asking him for affection and warmth, he is not only unable to respond, he is angered that his precious equilibrium has been disturbed.

A Father's Initiative

"Fred has been such a good provider and he's so respected," Mrs. Mary Davis explained to me in her bewilderment, "that I feel terrible about how I feel toward him. I get so very angry at him; then I feel so guilty I can't stand myself. I try to talk to him about how I feel about him and about the children. He becomes uncomfortable, clams up, then is mad at me. Then I'm upset and angry and try to get back at him—I even get frigid and can't make love with him. What can I do? I am so worried about my marriage and my children, but I can't even talk to my husband about it. How can our marriage last? We can't even talk and share our thoughts or feelings."

There's the old story. Mr. Davis is competent in the business world. He knows his business. He has the facts. Fred is comfortable in a world where emotional factors are omitted and generally not needed. He is "cognitive" in his communications. But home? Like a fish out of water. He's married to a very normal wife with very normal womanly and wifely needs. Mary needs her husband's warmth and support. She needs him to share in her concerns, fears, and hopes. Mary tends to be on the "emotional" side in her communications. She needs to feel her husband is willing to assume his responsibility for the family. These needs of hers are normal and do not mean that she is weak, overly sensitive, or that she is not carrying her own responsibilities. I have yet to see a truly happy, warm family where the husband and father did not assume family responsibility. Again, the wife and mother has her responsibilities, but the husband must be willing to help her and support her in each of these. One reason that this is essential is that a woman has a difficult time initiating love for her husband when she feels her husband is not willing to support her 100 percent in all areas of family life, emotional and otherwise. Of course, the same is true regarding the husband's family responsibility. He must know that his wife is ready to help and even step in when needed.

Another way to put it is that when a woman must assume responsibility because her husband simply has ignored it, that is, by default, it is hard for her to feel secure and comfortable in his love. For example, one lady whom I was counseling complained that she felt insecure in her husband's love and had difficulty responding to him lovingly. As it turned out, she was responsible strictly by default, for essentially every aspect of the family life including the yard and handling the finances. This arrangement may be all right if husband and wife both agree and are happy with it; but even then, the husband must assume that overall responsibility if needed; that is, he must be ready and willing to take over if the spouse is overburdened. A husband's "willingness" to be completely answerable for his family is one of the greatest assets a wife and child can have.

A wife can be wonderful at accepting love initiated by her husband, amplifying it manyfold, and reflecting it to him and the children, filling the home with an inexplicably wonderful climate. But the husband must take the responsibility of initiating love. Husbands who have found this secret are to be envied. The love returned to him by his wife is priceless, in my opinion the most precious commodity in this world. It is difficult to initiate love at first, but as the husband experiences his wife's love in return, he finds it to be multiplied many times, and sees that as this love increases with time, it becomes easier and easier to do.

If there are exceptions, I have yet to find one. The husband who will take full, total, overall responsibility for his family, and take the initiative in conveying his love to his wife and children, will experience unbelievable rewards: a loving, appreciative, helping wife who will be her loveliest for him; children who are safe, secure, content and able to grow to be their best. I personally have never seen marriage fail if these priorities are met. Every failing marriage I have seen has somehow missed these priorities. Fathers, the initiative must be ours.

But, you say to yourself, how can a husband take initiative and responsibility for conveying love in the family when he is essentially cognitive and clumsy in the feelings area, and the wife is more competent in the emotional area? My friend, you have just hit upon one of the most frequent, unrecognized, and difficult problems in marriage today. It is difficult to deal with, because most men, like Fred, are not aware of the problems. Instead of seeing how vital the emotional life of his wife and children is, he sees it as an uncomfortable nuisance which should be avoided. The result, of course, is what we just experienced between Fred and Mary, frustration and bewilderment with breakdown of communications.

It seems that everyone today realizes how crucial communications are in family living. Can you see from Fred and Mary's relationship how communications get bogged down when a "cognitive" husband cannot talk on the emotional level, or an "emotional" wife cannot share her innermost feelings and longings? What a dilemma! Husbands, we must face facts. The chances are overwhelming that our wives are more competent in the area of love, caring, and identifying emotional needs in us and our children. And we generally follow the guidance of experts, right? Then, clearly, we men desperately need our wives' help in leading us in this relatively foreign world of feeling.

Not only must we husbands be willing to respect and be guided by our wives' natural know-how in emotional areas, we must encourage her and support her daily task of setting the emotional climate in the home. If we are a hindrance to her, or perhaps even beset her in this, we will discourage her and eventually break her spirit. Oh, how many dear wives I have seen in counseling who have been thwarted by their husbands in efforts to feelingly love them and the children. These wives' spirits are broken, and the depression is crippling.

But look at marriages where a husband appreciates his wife's deep feelings and her need to communicate them. He not only listens to her, he learns from her. He learns how rewarding and profoundly fulfilling and satisfying it is to share on the emotional level, whether it is pleasant or unpleasant. This is a marriage that grows over the years. A husband and wife become closer and invaluable to each other. Such a marriage is one of life's greatest gifts.

Is Love Blind?

"See? He doesn't love me anymore. All he does is criticize me," complained pretty Yvonne. She and her husband John were seeing me "as a last resort" for marriage counseling. Yvonne continued, "Isn't there anything good you can say about me, John?" Much to my surprise, John actually could think of nothing with which to compliment his wife. Yvonne was attractive, intelligent, articulate, and talented, but John seemed only able to point out discrepancies. They had been married six years. Why the apparent inconsistency?

It's hard to realize, when we think of the astounding divorce rate, that essentially all marriages begin with great hope, expectation, love, and wonderful feelings between the newlyweds. Initially all seems wonderful, the world is perfect. And the marriage of Yvonne and John began that way too. What a startling change! How could it possibly have happened?

One factor is *immaturity*. But what is immaturity? It does correlate somewhat with age, but not necessarily. Within the scope of this particular problem, immaturity can be defined as the inability to tolerate (or cope with) ambivalence on a conscious level. Ambivalence is simply having opposite or conflicting feelings toward the same person.

This explains the saying, "love is blind." When we are first in love, and during the first weeks or months of our marriage, we must see our loved one as perfect, and we can tolerate no unpleasant feeling toward her/him. Therefore, we suppress (deny, ignore) anything we might not like in our spouse. We can then be aware of only his/her good points. Then we are oblivious to such things as an imperfect figure or physique, overtalkativeness, quietness, tendency to be fat or thin, overexuberance, withdrawal, moodiness, lack of ability in sports, music, art, sewing, or cooking.

This hiding of our spouse's undesirable aspects from ourselves works beautifully at first. As we live with our loved one day in, day out, month in, month out, there are new discoveries about him/her. Some good and some not so good. Some even revolting. But as long as we keep suppressing the unpleasant into our unconscious, we can continue to see our dear one as a near-perfect model, and everything is fine.

One problem. We cannot keep on suppressing forever. Someday we reach a point of saturation. At that time we may have been married several days or several years. This depends on (1) our capacity to suppress, overlook, and ignore the unpleasant, and (2) our level of maturity, namely, our ability to deal consciously with our mixed feelings.

When we reach this critical point, we cannot continue to suppress the negative any longer. Suddenly we are faced with days/months/years of disagreeable feelings toward our spouse. Again, because of immaturity (inability to deal with ambivalence), we do a flip-flop. We suppress the *good* feelings and accentuate the bad. Now we see our spouse in an almost reversed aspect of being all bad with little or no good. Overwhelmingly unpleasant or almost nothing pleasant.

And this can happen quickly. Two months ago John saw Yvonne as the epitome of perfection. Now he can barely tolerate her presence. Yvonne has remained essentially the same. John's perceptions of her have almost completely reversed.

How do we cope with this common problem that is plaguing our social structure and threatening the strength of our national fiber? As usual, the answer is easy to give, but difficult to carry out. First, we *must realize* that no one is perfect. It's amazing. We hear that statement every day, but we don't believe it. By playing the suppression game, we show that we want and expect perfection from our loved ones.

Second, we must keep ourselves continually aware of our spouse's assets and liabilities. I must realize and not forget that there are things about my wife for which I am grateful and things about her I wish were different—she's like all other women. It's taken me a long time to learn to think of her delightful traits during times when I'm disappointed with her.

Thirdly, we must learn to accept our spouses as they are, including their faults. The likelihood of finding someone or something better through divorce and another marriage, or in an affair, is remote, especially with the overwhelming guilt and other problems such action would produce. Remember that your wife or husband is truly irreplaceable.

Unconditional Love

"Love is very patient and kind, never jealous or envious, never boastful or proud, never haughty or selfish or rude. Love does not demand its own way. It is not irritable or touchy. It does not hold grudges and will hardly even notice when others do it wrong. It is never glad about injustice, but rejoices whenever truth wins out. If you love someone you will be loyal to him no matter what the cost. You will always believe in him, always expect the best of him, and always stand your ground in defending him" (1 Cor. 13:4-7, LB).

This clear statement tells us the foundation of all love relationships. The secret here can be called "unconditional love" that is not dependent on such things as spouse performance, age, weight, mistakes, etc. This kind of love says, "I love my wife, no matter what. No matter what she does, how she looks, or what she says. I will always love her." Yes, unconditional love is an ideal and impossible to attain completely, but the closer I can come to it, the more my wife will be made perfect by Him who loves us so. And the more He changes her to His likeness, the more pleasing she will be to me and the more I will be satisfied by her.

This brings us to the end of our discussion on marriage per se. We only touched a few points, but there are many fine books on the subject, and now we want to move on to our primary task of learning how to love a child.

As we explore the world of a child, we must remember that the marital relationship remains unquestionably the most important bond in a family. Its effect on a child throughout his life is tremendous.

One example from my experience which bears this out involves a Christian family I saw in counseling several months ago. Jennifer, a fifteen-year-old girl, was brought to me by her parents because of sexual misconduct which resulted in pregnancy. The child was a beautiful girl with a delightful personality. She was talented in several areas. Jennifer had a strong, warm, healthy relationship with her father—a somewhat scarce commodity these days. Her relationship with her mother also seemed sound. At first I was baffled why Jennifer chose to become sexually involved in the way she did. She had little feeling or concern about the boy who fathered the child. And she was not of a temperament which would inappropriately seek male attention. Jennifer had always been a respectful, compliant child who was easy for her parents to manage. Then why did Jennifer suddenly become pregnant? I was stumped.

Then I saw the parents together and individually. You guessed it. Jennifer's parents had marital conflicts that were well hidden from others. These strifes were of a longstanding nature, but the family managed to function for years in a fairly stable way. And Jennifer had always enjoyed a close relationship with her father. As the child grew older, the mother became increasingly jealous of this bond. But other than this jealousy, the Mother had a fairly supportive relationship with Jennifer.

Then Jennifer reached adolescence. As her physical features began changing into those of a woman, the mother's jealousy mushroomed. By various forms of nonverbal communication (which we will get into later), the mother relayed a message to Jennifer loud and clear. The message was that Jennifer was now a woman who could hereafter look after her own emotional needs, especially attention from the male population. As many girls of that age do, Jennifer attempted to substitute attention from male peers for her daddy's love. Jennifer was acting in accordance with her mother's subconscious, nonverbal instructions.

Her mother was aware of her own unhappy marital situation which resulted in a poor sexual life with her spouse. She was also aware of the closeness between Jennifer and her father. She was *not* aware of the intenseness of her jealousy toward Jennifer. And she was not aware of her role in Jennifer's sexual acting out.

In cases such as this, it is fruitless and many times harmful to confront each person, (especially the mother in this case) with fault or wrongdoing. Even though the surface complaint was the child's behavior, the basic problem was in the marital relationship. To help this family in the most supportive, loving, sensitive way, the therapist must help the parents in their marriage bond and not focus on faultfinding and judging their mistakes. He must also uphold God's forgiveness in offering relief from true guilt in the matter. As the marital bond is mended, and guilt is resolved, this troubled mother-child relationship can be rectified.

This case illustration should show how important is the marital union in the life of a child. The stronger and healthier this bond is, the fewer problems we will encounter as parents. And the more effective will be the information in this book when it is applied.

Let's look now at the second most important relationship in the family.

3

The Foundation

Real love is unconditional, and should be evident in all love relationships (see 1 Corinthians 13:4-7). The foundation of a solid relationship with our child is unconditional love. Only that type of love relationship can assure a child's growth to his full and total potential. Only this foundation of unconditional love can assure prevention of problems such as feelings of resentment, being unloved, guilt, fear, insecurity.

We can be confident that a child is correctly disciplined only if our primary relationship with him is one of unconditional love. Without a basis of unconditional love it is not possible to understand a child, his behavior, or to know how to deal with misbehavior.

Unconditional love can be viewed as a guiding light in child rearing. Without it, we parents will be operating in the dark with no daily landmarks to tell us where we are and what we should do regarding our child. With it, we have indicators of where we are, where the child is, and what to do in all areas, including discipline. Only with this foundation do we have a cornerstone on which to build our expertise in guiding our child and filling his needs on a daily basis. Without a foundation of unconditional love, parenting is a confusing and frustrating burden.

What is unconditional love? Unconditional love is loving a child *no matter what*. No matter what the child looks like. No matter what his assets, liabilities, handicaps. No matter what we expect him to be and most difficult, no matter how he acts. This does not mean, of course, that we always like his behavior. Unconditional love means we love the *child* even when at times we may detest his behavior.

As we mentioned when discussing unconditional love in the marriage relationship, it is an ideal which we will never achieve 100 percent of the time. But, again, the closer we get to it, and the more we achieve it, the more satisfied and confident parents we will become. And the more satisfied, pleasant, and happy will be our child.

How I wish I could say, "I love my children all the time regardless of anything else, including their behavior." But like all parents, I cannot. Yet I will give myself credit for trying to arrive at that wonderful goal of loving them unconditionally. I do this by constantly reminding myself that:

(1) they are children

(2) they will tend to act like children

(3) much of childish behavior is unpleasant

(4) if I do my part as a parent and love them despite their childish behavior, they will be able to mature and give up childish ways

(5) if I only love them when they please me (conditional love), and convey my love to them only during those times, they will not feel genuinely loved. This in turn will make them insecure, damage their self-image, and actually *prevent* them from moving on to better self-control and more mature behavior. Therefore, their behavior and its development is *my* responsibility as much as theirs

(6) if I love them unconditionally, they will feel good about themselves and be comfortable with themselves. They will then be able to control their anxiety and, in turn, their behavior, as they grow into adulthood

(7) if I only love them when they meet my requirements or

expectations, they will feel incompetent. They will believe it is fruitless to do their best because it is never enough. Insecurity, anxiety, and low self-esteem will plague them. They will be constant hindrances in their emotional and behavioral growth. Again, their total growth is as much my responsibility as theirs

(8) for my sake as a struggling parent, and for my sons' (and daughter's) sakes, I pray my love for my children will be as unconditional as I can make it. The future of my children depends on this foundation.

A Child and His Feelings
Remember the simple graph in Chapter 2? Where do you think we would find children on it? Right! Way over on the left side. A child comes into the world with an amazing ability to perceive emotionally. The child is so sensitive to the feelings of his mother. It is a beautiful thing to see a newborn infant brought to his mother for the first time, if the mother truly wants him. He conforms to the mother's body and his contentment is obvious to all.

But a child's first meeting with a mother who does not want him presents another picture. This poor child is not content and frequently nurses poorly, frets a great deal, and is obviously unhappy. This can frequently be seen when the mother is troubled or depressed, even though no difference in his treatment by the mother can be discerned.

So it is very important to realize that from birth, children are extremely sensitive emotionally. Since their fund of knowledge is of course small, their way of communicating with their world is primarily on the feeling level. This is crucial. Do you see it? A child's first impressions of the world are through his feelings. This is wonderful yet frightening when we think of the importance of it. A child's emotional being determines how he sees his world—his parents, his home, himself.

This sets the stage and foundation for almost everything else. For example, if a child sees his world as rejecting, unloving, uncaring, hostile, then what I consider a child's greatest enemy—

anxiety—will be harmful to his speech, behavior, ability to relate and to learn. The point is that a child is not only emotionally supersensitive but also vulnerable.

Almost every study I know indicates that any child is continually asking his parents, "Do you love me?" A child asks this emotional question mostly in his behavior, seldom verbally. The answer to this question is absolutely the most important thing in any child's life.

"Do you love me?" If we love a child unconditionally, he feels the answer to the question is yes. If we love him conditionally, he is unsure, and, again, prone to anxiety. The answer we give a child to this all-important question, "Do you love me?" pretty well determines his basic attitude toward life. It's crucial.

A child usually asks us this question with his behavior, and so we give him our answer by our behavior. Not only by what we say, but by what we do. By this behavior, a child tells us what he *needs,* whether it's more love, more discipline, more acceptance, or more understanding. (We'll get into this in detail later, but right now let's concentrate on the irreplaceable foundation of unconditional love.)

By our behavior, we meet these needs but we can do this only if our relationship is founded on unconditional love. I hope you caught the phrase "by our behavior." The feeling of love for a child in our heart may be strong. But it is not enough. By our behavior does a child see our love for him. Our love for a child is conveyed by our behavior toward that child, by what we *say* and what we *do.* But what we do carries more weight. A child is far more affected by our actions than by our words. We'll get into how to do it soon.

Another critical concept for parents to understand is that each child has an *emotional tank.* This tank is figurative, of course, but very real. Each child has certain emotional needs, and whether these emotional needs are met (through love, understanding, discipline, etc) determines many things. First of all, how a child feels: whether he is content, angry, depressed, or joyful. Secondly, it affects his behavior: whether he is obedient, disobedient, whiny, perky, playful, or withdrawn. Naturally, the fuller the tank, the more positive the feelings and the better the behavior.

At this point let me make one of the most important statements in this book. *Only if the emotional tank is full, can a child be expected to be at his best or to do his best.* And whose responsibility is it to keep that emotional tank full? You guessed it, the parents'. A child's behavior indicates the status of the tank. Later we'll talk about how to fill the tank, but now let's understand that this tank has got to be kept full and only we parents can really do it. Only if the tank is kept full, can a child really be happy, reach his potential, and respond appropriately to discipline. God, help me to meet my child's need as you do mine. "And my God will meet all your needs" (Phil. 4:19, NIV).

Children Reflect Love

Children may be conceptualized as mirrors. They reflect, but do not initiate love. If love is given to them, they return it. If none is given, they have none to return. Unconditional love is reflected unconditionally, and conditional love is returned conditionally.

The love between Tom and his parents is an example of a conditional relationship. As Tom was growing up, he yearned for a close, warm relationship with his parents. Unfortunately his parents felt that they should continually prompt him to do better by withholding praise, warmth, and affection except for truly outstanding behavior, when he made them feel proud. Otherwise, they were strict, in that they felt too much approval and affection would spoil him and dampen his striving to be better. Their love was given when Tom excelled, but was withheld otherwise. This probably worked well when Tom was very young. But as he grew older, he began feeling that his parents really didn't love or appreciate him in his own right, but cared only about their own esteem.

By the time Tom became a teenager, his love for his parents strongly resembled that of his parents for him. He had learned well how to love conditionally. He only behaved in a way which pleased his parents when his parents did something to please him. Of course, with both Tom and his parents playing this game, eventually neither could convey love to the other because each was waiting for the other to do something pleasing. In this situation, each one becomes more and more disappointed, confused, and bewildered. Eventually depression, anger, and resentment set in, prompting the Smiths to seek help.

How would you handle that situation? Some would instruct the parents to demand their rights as parents: respect, obedience, etc. Some would criticize Tom for his attitude toward his parents and demand that he honor them. Some would recommend severe punishment for Tom. Think about it.

Many children today do not feel genuinely loved by their parents. And yet, I've met few parents who do not love them dearly. This is not just an academic question to think about and then say, "That's too bad." The situation is alarming. Dozens of religious cults or other devious organizations are capturing the minds of thousands of our precious young people all over the nation. How can these children so easily be brainwashed, turned against their parents and all other authority, and controlled by such bizarre doctrines? The main reason is that these young people have never felt truly loved and cared for by their parents. They feel that they were deprived of something, that their parents missed giving them something. What is it? Yes, unconditional love. When you consider how few children really feel properly cared for, loved, and comfortable, it is no wonder how far these groups can go.

Why does this terrible situation exist? I do not believe parents per se should be blamed. When I talk to parents I am gratified to find that most not only love their children, but are genuinely interested in what can be done to help *all* children. I find over and over again that the problem is parents do not know how to *convey* their love to their children.

I am not pessimistic. As I lecture around the country, I am very heartened that today's parents not only listen, but are willing to expend themselves and their resources on behalf of their children. Many have changed their relationship with their children so that it is founded on scripturally based unconditional love. They have found that once this has been accomplished, their children's emotional tanks are filled for the first time. Parenting then becomes fulfilling, exciting, and rewarding. Then these fine parents have guidelines as to when and how to guide and discipline their dear ones.

How to Convey Love

Let's consider how to convey love to a child. As you remember, children are emotional beings who communicate emotionally. In addition, children (and the younger, the more so) use behavior to translate their feelings to us. It's easy to tell how a child is feeling and what frame of mind he's in simply by watching him. Likewise, children have an uncanny ability to recognize our feelings by our behavior, an ability most people lose as they reach adulthood.

On many occasions my 16-year-old daughter has asked me such questions as, "What are you mad at, Daddy?" when I'm not even consciously aware that I'm feeling a certain way. But when I stop and think about it, she's absolutely right.

Children are that way. They can so finely sense how you are feeling by the way you act. So if we want them to know how we feel *about them,* that we love them, *we must act like we love them,* "Dear children, let us not love with words or tongue but with actions and in truth" (1 John 3:18, NIV).

The purpose of the book is to examine how parents can put their feelings of love into action. Only in this way can they convey their love to their child so that he will feel loved, completely accepted, and respected, and able to love and respect himself. Only then will parents be able to help their children to love others unconditionally, especially their future spouses and children.

Before we launch into discoveries of how to love a child, there must be one presupposition. It must be assumed that parents love their child. That is, it must be assumed that parents are willing to apply what they learn. There is a difference between having a vague feeling of warmth toward a child, and caring enough about him to sacrifice whatever is needed for his best interest. It is rather pointless to continue reading the book if you are not willing to seriously contemplate what it says, understand it, and apply its contents. Otherwise, it would be easy to read it superficially and to disown the information as simplistic and unrealistic.

Conveying love to a child can be broadly classified into four areas: eye contact, physical contact, focused attention, and discipline. Each area is just as crucial as the other. Many parents (and authorities) will focus on one or two areas and neglect the others. The area most overemphasized today, to the exclusion of the rest, is discipline. I see many children of Christian parents who are well-disciplined but feel unloved. In many of these cases the parents have unfortunately confused discipline with punishment, as though the two are synonymous. This is understandable when one reads books and articles and attends seminars on the subject. I frequently read or hear authorities tell parents to use the rod and physically pinch their child with no mention of loving him. There is no mention of how to help a child feel good toward himself, his parents, or others. No mention of how to make a child happy.

Every day I see the results of this approach to childrearing. These children are well-behaved when they are quite young, although usually overly quiet, somewhat sullen, and withdrawn. They lack the spontaneity, curiosity, and childish exuberance of a love-nurtured child. And these children usually become behavior problems as they approach and enter adolescence because they lack a strong emotional bond with their parents.

So we parents must focus on all areas of loving our child. Let's move on and discuss the first one, namely, eye contact.

4

How to Love Your Child —Eye Contact

When you first think about eye contact, it seems relatively unimportant in relating to your child. However, as we work with children, observe communications between parent and child, and study research findings, we realize how essential eye contact is. Eye contact is crucial not only in making good communicational contact with a child, but in filling his emotional needs. Without realizing it, we use eye contact as a primary means of conveying love, especially to children. A child uses eye contact with his parents (and others) to feed emotionally. The more parents make eye contact with their child as a means of expressing their love, the more a child is nourished with love and the fuller is his emotional tank.

What is eye contact? Eye contact is looking directly into the eyes of another person. Most people do not realize how crucial eye contact is. Have you ever tried to have a conversation with someone who keeps looking in another direction, unable to maintain eye contact with you? It's difficult. And our feelings toward that person are very much affected by this. We tend to like people who are able to maintain pleasant eye contact with us. Eye contact is pleasant, of course, when it is accompanied by pleasant words and pleasant facial expressions, like smiling.

Unfortunately, parents, without realizing it, can use eye contact to give other messages to their child. For instance, parents may give loving eye contact only under certain conditions, as when a child performs especially well and brings pride to his parents. This comes across to a child as conditional love. As we mentioned in the last chapter, a child cannot grow and develop well under these circumstances. Even though we may love a child deeply, we must give him appropriate eye contact. Otherwise, he will get the wrong message and will not feel genuinely (unconditionally) loved.

It is easy for parents to develop the terrible habit of using eye contact primarily when they want to make a strong point to a child, especially a negative one. We find that a child is most attentive when we look him straight in the eye. We may do this mainly to give instructions or for reprimanding and criticizing. This is a *disastrous* mistake. This method of using eye contact primarily in the negative sense works well when a child is quite young.

But remember that eye contact is one of the main sources of a child's emotional nurturing. When a parent uses this powerful means of control at his disposal in a primarily negative way, a child cannot but see his parent in a primarily negative way. And though this may seem to have good results when a child is young, this child is obedient and docile because of fear. As he grows older, the fear gives way to anger, resentment, and depression. Reread Tom's statements: this is what he is telling us.

Oh, if his parents had only known! They loved Tom deeply, but they were unaware that they seldom gave him eye contact, and when they did, it was when they wanted to give him explicit instructions or when disciplining him. Tom inherently knew that his parents somehow loved him. But, because of this way of using the critical ingredient of eye contact, Tom has always been confused and bewildered regarding his parents' true feelings toward him. Remember his statement, "No one cares about me except my friends"? When I replied, "No one?", he said, "My parents, I guess. I don't know." Tom knows he should feel loved, but he does not.

An even worse habit parents may get into is actually using the avoidance of eye contact as a punishment device. This is cruel and we often do this to our spouses. (Come on, admit it.) Consciously refusing to make eye contact with a child is usually more painful than corporal punishment. It can be devastating. It can be one of those incidents in a child's life that he will never forget.

There are several types of circumstances between parent and child which can have lifelong effects, happenings that a child, and sometimes a parent, never forgets. The purposeful withdrawing of eye contact from a child as a way to show disapproval can be such a time and is obviously an example of conditional love. A wise parent will do all in his power to avoid it.

Our ways of showing love to a child should not be controlled by our being pleased or displeased. We must show our love consistently, unwaveringly, no matter what the situation. We can take care of misbehavior in other ways—ways which will not interfere with our love-giving. We'll talk about discipline and how to do it without disrupting the love-bond. What we must understand at this point is that parents must use eye contact as a continuous love-giving route, and not merely as a means of discipline.

We Are Patterns

We all know that children learn by role modeling, that is, patterning themselves after us. Children learn the art and use of eye contact this way also. If we give a child continuous, loving, positive eye contact, he will do the same. If we use eye contact as a way to display our annoyances, he will also.

Do you know a child who seems to be unpleasant or even obnoxious? Most likely he will look at you for only a brief period of time when he first sees you, and thereafter only when you have something particularly interesting to say or do. Other than that, he avoids looking at you. This fleeting eye contact is annoying, obnoxious, and can be aggravating. Now observe the way this child's parents use eye contact with him. Is there a similarity?

Imagine the distinct disadvantage this child has and will have throughout his life. Imagine how difficult it will be to develop friendships and other intimate relationships. How rejected and disliked he will be by his peers, not only now but probably indefinitely because the chances of his breaking this pattern of relating are bleak. First of all, he is not aware he's doing it, and secondly, changing this pattern is extraordinarily difficult, *unless the parents change their own pattern of eye contact before the child becomes too old.* This is a child's best hope.

A perfect example of this tragedy was discovered in a research study on a pediatric ward in a general hospital. The researcher was sitting at one end of the corridor recording the number of times the nurses and volunteers entered each child's room. It was noted that some children were visited many times more often than others. The reasons were startling. It had something to do with the type of seriousness of the child's illness, of course, and with the amount of care required by the child. But this did not explain the great differences in the amount of contact with the patients. You've probably guessed it. The more popular child received more attention. Whenever nurses or volunteers had a free moment or a choice between which room to enter, they naturally picked the child who could relate in the most pleasant way.

What made the difference in how pleasant the child was? There were several reasons, such as alertness, verbal ability, and spontaneity, but the most consistent factor was eye contact. The least popular children would initially look at the visitor briefly, then immediately look down or away. Subsequently the children would avoid eye contact, making it difficult to relate to them. The adults would naturally be uncomfortable with these children. The nurses or volunteers, not realizing their roles in initiating communication, would misunderstand them, assuming that the children wanted to be alone, or that the children did not like them. Consequently these children were avoided, making them feel even more unloved, unwanted, and worthless.

This same thing happens in thousands of homes. It happened

in Tom's. And it could have been corrected with continuous, warm, pleasant eye contact (unconditional love) by the parents. If they had known this (and some other basic facts about loving children which we'll proceed to), they wouldn't have had these problems with their boy.

The Failure to Thrive Syndrome

Another important finding in our research studies also took place in a pediatric ward, but at a university hospital. We were studying the strange phenomenon of the Failure to Thrive Syndrome. In this illness, a child, usually between 6 and 12 months of age, ceases to develop. Often he stops eating and growing, becomes listless and lethargic, and may actually die for no apparent reason. All tests and physical examinations are normal. Why does a child lose his will to live? In most cases we know that the parents have rejected the child, often unconsciously (outside of their awareness). They are unable consciously to deal with their feelings of rejection toward their child, so unconsciously, they reject him through their behavior. These parents were found avoiding eye contact and physical contact with their child. Otherwise, we found them to be doing their job as parents, providing food, clothing, etc.

The Failure to Thrive Syndrome is a startling phenomenon, but other findings are even more so. During the World War II Nazi blitzes of London, many young children were removed for their protection from the city and placed with adults in the countryside. Their parents remained in London. These children were basically well cared for physically, in that they were clean, well fed, and comfortable. Emotionally, however, they were severely deprived because there were not enough caretakers to give the emotional nurturing of eye contact and physical contact.

Most of these children were emotionally disturbed and handicapped. It would have been far better to have kept them with their mothers. The danger of emotional damage was greater than the danger of physical damage.

The danger and pitfalls awaiting an emotionally weak child are frightening. Parents! Make your children strong. Your greatest tool is unconditional love.

Eye Contact and the Learning Process

In my work with the Headstart Program, I love to teach those wonderful teachers about eye contact and physical contact and how these affect anxiety and a child's ability to learn.

A teacher will identify a three-to-four-year-old child who is obviously anxious, fearful, and immature by the difficulty he has in making or maintaining eye contact. Mild to moderate emotional deprivation can cause a child to have difficulty with eye contact.

The extremely anxious child will, in addition, have problems approaching an adult (and often his peers). A normally emotionally nourished child will be able to approach the teacher by walking directly up to her, making full non-hesitating eye contact, and speaking what's on his mind—for instance, "May I have a piece of paper?" The more emotionally deprived a child is, the more difficulty he will have in doing this.

In the average schoolroom it is not hard to find at least one child (usually a boy) who is so anxious and fearful that he cannot make good eye contact, speaks with great hesitancy (and frequently cannot speak without coaxing), and will approach his teacher with a side or oblique approach. Occasionally the child will only be able to approach his teacher walking almost backwards. Of course these children have difficulty learning because they are so anxious and tense.

When we have found such an unfortunate child, I ask the teacher to teach him something while sitting across the table from him. Then I ask the teacher to hold the child, make occasional eye contact with him (as much as the child can tolerate) while talking with him. After a short while, I again ask the teacher to teach the child something while continuing to hold him. The teacher is amazed, and I am always amazed, at how much easier it is for the child to learn when his emotional needs are cared for first. With eye contact and physical contact, the teacher has eased the child's fears and anxiety, and increased his sense of security and confidence. This, in turn, enables him to learn better. Simple? Of course. Then why don't we do it more? For many reasons, I believe, ranging from a fear that we'll appear unprofessional, or fearing we'll spoil a child, to fearing we'll somehow damage him in some vague way. If there is anything we don't have to worry about, it's giving a child too much love.

In a New Place

I am so thankful as a parent that I learned about the importance of eye contact. It has made a great difference with my own children. I'll never forget for example, when we first moved to our present home. Our two boys were six and two at the time and were happy, energetic, and normally independent.

About a week after moving, we noticed a change coming over both boys. They were becoming whiny, clinging, easily upset, frequently fighting, constantly underfoot, and irritable. At that time, my wife Pat and I were furiously trying to get the house ready before I was to report to my new job. We were both becoming annoyed and irritated with the boys' behavior, but figured it was because of the move.

One night I was thinking about my boys and I had the idea of imagining myself in their place. The answer to their behavioral problems suddenly hit me like a hammer. Pat and I were with the boys night and day and talked to them frequently. But we were so intent on the housework that we never really gave them their rightful attention, we never made eye contact and seldom made physical contact. Their emotional tanks had run dry, and *by their behavior* they were asking, "Do you love me?" In their childlike, normally irrational way, they were asking, "Do you love me now that we're in a new place? Are things still the same with us? Do you still love me?" So typical of children during a time of change.

As soon as I understood the problem, I shared my thoughts with Pat. I think she was a bit incredulous at first, but by then she was ready to try anything.

The next day we gave the boys eye contact whenever we

could, when they talked to us (active listening) and when we talked to them. Whenever possible, we held them and gave them concentrated attention. The change was dramatic. As their emotional tanks were filled, they became their happy, radiant, rambunctious selves and soon were spending less time underfoot and more time playing with each other and keeping themselves happy. Pat and I agreed that this was time well spent. We more than made up for it when the boys were out from underfoot, but more important, they were happy again.

It's Never Too Early

Let me give you one more illustration regarding the importance of eye contact. An infant's eyes begin focusing somewhere around two and four weeks of age. One of the first images which holds an infant's attention is a human face, but in particular he focuses on the eyes.

After a child is approximately six to eight weeks of age, you will notice that his eyes are always moving and seem to be searching for something. The eyes resemble two radar antennae constantly moving and searching. Do you know what he's looking for? I think you already know: he's searching for another set of eyes. As early as two months, these eyes lock on another set of eyes. Already he is feeding emotionally, and even at this very early age his emotional tank needs to be filled.

Awesome, isn't it? It's no wonder that a child's way of relating to his world, and his feelings toward it, are so well formed early in his life. Most researchers state that a child's basic personality, modes of thinking, style of speech, and other critical traits are well fixed by the age of five.

We cannot start too early in giving a child continuous, warm, consistent affection. He simply *must* have this unconditional love to cope most effectively in today's world. And we have a simple but extremely powerful method by which to give it to him. But eye contact can be used wrongly as a device to control, as we discussed previously. It's up to each parent to use eye contact to convey unconditional love.

5

How to Love Your Child —Physical Contact

It seems that the most obvious way of conveying our love to a child is by physical contact. Surprisingly, studies show that most parents touch their children only when necessity demands it, as when helping them to dress, undress, or get into the car. Otherwise few parents take advantage of this pleasant, effortless way of giving their children that unconditional love they so desperately need. You seldom see a parent on his own volition or "out of the blue" take an opportunity to touch his child.

I don't mean just hugging, kissing, and the like. I'm also talking about any type of physical contact. It is such a simple thing to touch a child on his shoulder, gently poke him in the ribs, or tousle his hair. When you closely observe parents with their children, many actually attempt to make the least possible physical contact. It's as if these poor parents have the notion their children are like mechanical walking dolls, the object being to get them walking and behaving correctly with the least assistance. These parents don't know the fantastic opportunities they are missing. Within their hands they have a way of assuring their children's emotional security and their own success as parents.

It is heartening to see some parents who have discovered this secret of physical contact along with eye contact.

Last summer my eight-year-old son played Peanut League Baseball, and I sat on the bleachers to watch him play. During the games I especially enjoyed watching one father who had discovered the secrets of eye and physical contact. Frequently his boy would run up to tell him something. It was obvious that there was a strong affectional bond between them. As they talked, their eye contact was direct with no hesitation. And their communication included much appropriate physical contact, especially when something funny was said. This father would frequently lay his hand on his son's arm, or put his arm around his son's shoulder and sometimes slap him on the knee. Occasionally, he would pat him on the back or pull the child toward him, especially when a humorous comment was made. You could tell that this father used physical contact whenever he possibly could, as long as he and the boy were comfortable and it was appropriate.

Occasionally, this same father's teenage daughter would come to watch her brother play. She would sit with her father, either at his side or directly in front of him. Here again, this caring and knowledgeable father related to his daughter in an appropriate manner. He used much eye and physical contact but because of her age, did not hold her on his lap or kiss her (as he would have done if she were younger). He would frequently lightly touch her hand, arm, shoulder, or back. Occasionally he would tap her on the knee or briefly put his arm around her shoulder and lightly jerk her toward him, especially when something funny happened.

Two Precious Gifts
Physical and eye contact are to be incorporated in all of our everyday dealings with our children. They should be natural, comfortable, and not showy or overdone. A child growing up in a home where parents use eye and physical contact will be comfortable with himself and other people. He will have an easy time communicating with others, and consequently be well liked and have good self-esteem. Appropriate and frequent eye and physical contact are two of the most precious gifts we can give our child.

Eye and physical contact (along with focused attention, see chapter 6) are the most effective ways to fill a child's emotional tank and enable him to be his best.

Unfortunately, Tom's parents had not discovered the secret of physical and eye contact. We found in the last chapter how they misused eye contact. They felt physical contact was all right for girls because "they needed affection." But Mr. and Mrs. Smith believed boys should be treated as men. They felt affection would feminize Tom into being a sissy. These grieving parents did not realize that the opposite is true, that the more Tom's emotional needs are met by physical and eye contact, especially by his father, the more he will identify with the male sex, and the more masculine he will be.

Mr. and Mrs. Smith also thought that as a boy gets older, his need for affection, especially physical affection, ceases. Actually a boy's need for physical contact never ceases, even though the type of physical contact he needs does change.

As an infant, he needs to be held, cuddled, fondled, hugged, and kissed; "ooey-gooey love stuff" my eight-year-old son calls it. This type of physical affection is crucial from birth until the boy reaches seven or eight years of age—and I mean crucial! Research shows that girl infants less than 12 months old receive five times as much physical affection as boy infants. I am convinced that this is one reason younger boys (three years to adolescence) have many more problems than girls. Five to six times as many boys as girls are seen in psychiatric clinics around the country. This ratio changes dramatically during adolescence.

It is apparent then how important it is for a boy to receive just as much affection (and often a boy needs more) as girls during the early years. As a boy grows and becomes older, his need for physical affection such as hugging and kissing lessens but his need for physical contact does not. Instead of primarily "ooey-gooey love stuff," he now wants "boy-style" physical contact such as playful wrestling, jostling, backslapping, playful hitting or boxing, bearhugs, "give-me-five" (slapping another person's palm in a moment of triumph). These ways of making physical contact with a boy are just as genuine a means of giving attention as hugging and kissing. Don't forget that a child *never* outgrows his need for *both* types.

As my boys get older, and they become less and less receptive to holding, hugging, and kissing, there are still times when they need it and want it and I must be alert in order to give this to them every chance I get. These times occur usually when they have been hurt (either physically or emotionally), when they are very tired, when they are sick, and at special periods such as bedtime or when something sad has happened.

Remember the special moments discussed in chapter 4? Moments that are especially meaningful to a child, so meaningful that he will *never forget* them? These special opportunities to give our children affectionate physical contact (hugging, kissing), *especially as they get older,* are some of these very special times. These are the moments your child will recall when he or she is in the throes of deepest adolescence, when a teenager is in the conflict of rebellion on one hand versus affection for his parents on the other. The more special memories he has, the stronger he will be able to stand against adolescent turmoil.

These precious opportunities are limited in number. A child quickly passes from one stage to the next and before we know it, opportunities to give him what he needs have come and gone. Somber thought, isn't it?

One other point I'd like to make about giving physical affection to boys. It is easier to give affection to a boy when he is younger, especially around 12 to 18 months of age. As he grows older, however, it becomes more difficult. Why? One reason, as we mentioned before, is the false assumption that the physical display of affection is feminine. The reason which I'd like to state here is that most boys become less appealing to people as they grow older. For example, to many people a seven or eight-year-old boy is unappealing, irritating, and often grotesque. In order to give a boy what he must have emotionally we must recognize these unpleasant feelings in ourselves, resist them, and go ahead with what we must do as mothers and fathers.

Let's talk about girls and their needs now. Girls generally do not display as much directness as boys to emotional deprivation during their first seven or eight years. In other words, they do not make their affectional needs so evident. I've seen many, many emotionally deprived children and, generally, it is very easy to tell which boys are suffering—their distress is usually obvious. But the girls seem better able to cope and are less affected by the lack of emotional nurturing *prior* to adolescence. Don't let this fool you. Although girls don't show their misery as much when they are younger, they suffer intensely when not properly cared for emotionally. It becomes quite evident as they grow older, especially during adolescence.

One reason for this lies in this matter of physical contact. Remember that physical contact, especially the more affectionate type (holding, hugging, kissing, etc.), is vital to boys during their younger years. The younger the boy, the more vital affectional contact is to him. While, with a girl, physical contact (especially the more affectionate type) *increases* in importance as she becomes older and reaches a zenith at around the age of eleven. Nothing stirs my heart more than an eleven-year-old girl who is not receiving adequate emotional nourishment. What a critical age!

Sharon's Personality Change

"I can't believe it! Sharon must be a Dr. Jekyll and Mr. Hyde," exclaimed Mrs. Francisco in her first visit with me concerning her fifteen-year-old daughter. "She has always been a quiet, shy girl who never really acted up. In fact, she had to be prompted to do things, especially over the last few months. For a while I couldn't get her to do anything. She seemed bored with life. She lost interest in everything, especially her school work. She seemed to lose all her energy. I took Sharon to her pediatrician but he couldn't find anything wrong with her. Then I talked to the school counselor and her teachers. They were also concerned with Sharon's attitude and boredom. Some friends told me not to worry, that it was a stage she'd grow out of. I hoped they were right but had my doubts. Then one day a friend of mine who has a daughter Sharon's age called. She said that her daughter thought Sharon was on drugs. I didn't think Sharon was the type but I searched her room anyway and found some marijuana.

"For the first time in her life she acted horribly. She yelled and screamed at me, saying I was prowling and I had no right to intrude on her privacy. I was shocked at her defiance.

"That seemed to be the beginning of her personality change. Now she's angry all the time, just hateful. She demands to go out with the worst crowd in school, and it scares me to think of what they might be doing.

"Now all she cares about is being away from home with her gooney friends. What will become of her, Dr. Campbell? We can't control her."

"Is Sharon the same way with her father?" I asked.

"She's much better with him for some reason, but even he is finding it more and more difficult to reason with her. But he's not around much to help anyway. He's so busy. Gone most of the time. Even when he's here, he doesn't give us much time. The children adore him and want to be with him. But he immediately finds something they have done wrong and gets on to them about it. He really cares about the kids. I know he does. But that's his way."

A tragic story. But a common one. A normal, well-endowed girl who for almost thirteen years was open, docile, easy to love. Like any child, her main concern was, "Do you love me?" For almost thirteen years her parents had nearly continuous opportunity to answer her question and prove their love to her. As a typical girl, her need for demonstrable love increased over the years and hit a maximum around the age of eleven—that ultra-critical age when girls have an almost desperate need for abundant eye contact, focused attention, and notably physical contact, especially from their fathers.

Preparation for Adolescence
Why is affectionate love so important to girls around that age of

pre-adolescence? The answer: preparation for adolescence. Every girl enters adolescence with some degree of preparation for it. Some are well prepared and some are poorly prepared.

The two most important aspects of this preparation for girls are self-image and sexual identity. At this point, let's look at sexual identity in a growing girl. As we mentioned before, a girl's need for affection increases as she grows older. As she nears adolescence she intuitively or unconsciously knows that how she weathers those turbulent adolescent years depends on how she feels about herself. It is vital for her to feel OK about herself as a female. If she is comfortable as a "woman" when she enters adolescence (usually about 13 to 15 years old), her adolescence will be relatively smooth, pleasant, and comfortable with the usual ups and downs. The more stable and healthy her sexual identity, the better she will be able to withstand peer pressure. The less well she thinks of herself as an "OK female," the less stable she will be. She will then be more susceptible to pressure of peers (especially male peers) and less able to hold to parental values.

Sexual identity is self-approval as a female, and a girl gets her sexual identity at that age primarily from her father, as long as he is living and especially if he is in the home. If a father is dead or otherwise removed from relating to his daughter, a girl must find other paternal figures to fill these needs. But when a father has any viable relationship with her, he is the primary person who can help his daughter be prepared in this particular way for adolescence. What a great responsibility!

A father helps his daughter to approve of herself by showing her that he himself approves of her. He does this by applying the principles we have discussed thus far—unconditional love, eye contact, and physical contact, as well as focused attention. A daughter's need for her father to do this begins as early as two years of age. This need, although important at younger ages, becomes greater as the girl grows older and approaches that almost magic age of thirteen.

One problem in our society is that as a girl grows older, a father usually feels increasingly uncomfortable about giving his daughter the affection she needs, especially when she becomes pre-adolescent (about 10 or 11 years old). So as a daughter arrives at the age when she needs her father's affection the most, a father feels more awkward and uncomfortable, especially with physical contact. This is extremely unfortunate. Fathers, we must ignore our discomfort and give our daughters what is vital to them for their entire lives.

Our Juvenile Court Judge

Like most fathers, I have my difficulties giving my children everything they need emotionally—especially physical contact for my teenage daughter, and focused attention. Most evenings I come home from work physically and emotionally exhausted. After expending myself in my work, how can I find the energy and resources to give to my family, especially my daughter, at those times when they need me? With my own daughter, her need for me lately has been occurring when she has had a bad encounter with her peer group, perhaps another girl being hostile toward her because of jealousy. Sometimes she doesn't understand the cause of the jealousy and tries to find the fault in herself. On occasions such as this, I know what I *should* do. I should go to her room, talk with her about whatever is on her mind at the moment, give her all the eye and physical contact she needs at this time, and patiently wait until she gets around to sharing with me her pain and confusion. Then I can clarify her understanding of the situation. After a while the fact finally dawns on her that it wasn't anything she had done wrong or should blame herself for. Then she usually sees the situation clearly enough to avoid similar difficulties.

Anyway, that's the way I'd *like* it to go, but as I said, I'm seldom bursting with energy and enthusiasm to carry it out. Usually all I feel like doing is eating supper, sitting in my favorite chair, reading the newspaper, and relaxing.

Let me tell you what has helped me overcome this inertia. When my daughter (or one of my sons) needs me, and my whole body is drawn like a magnet to a chair or bed, I think of my friend, our fine judge of the Juvenile Court. I deeply appreciate and respect the judge. One of the worst, most humiliating and tragic things that could possibly happen to me or my family would be to appear in his court with one of my children on, say, a drug charge. I say to myself, "Campbell, one out of every six kids appears before the Juvenile Court. If you want to make sure one of your kids isn't included, you'd better hop to it and give them what they need instead of looking after yourself." Just the thought of appearing before the judge with my child on some sort of charge is unbearable. It usually works. I get off my caboose and do what I know I must do as a father.

Back to physical contact. I was thinking about the importance of it one day. I was thinking how essential it is and yet how most parents seem to consider it so basic and simplistic; we assume we are doing it when, in fact, we seldom do. I was trying to think of an illustration to point out this problem when my dear wife ran across an unusual article in *The Saturday Evening Post* (August, 1976). The article was about religious cults, including the Unification Church (Moonies). One young man who was interviewed, told of being brainwashed by the Moonies.

One of the most powerful techniques was used as follows. In an emotionally charged atmosphere and surrounded by several Moonies, the young man was required to think back into his childhood and remember painful moments. He told of an incident when he was three years old. He remembered feeling lonely and distressed, and tried to seek comfort in physical contact from his mother. His mother did not have time for him at that moment and he felt rejected. Then the Moonies embraced him (physical contact) repeatedly, stating that *they* loved him (implying of course that his mother did not).

Frightening, isn't it? The fact that there are dozens of such religious cults in our country today trying to capture the minds of our children is alarming enough. But even worse is that they are able to do so because parents are failing to provide for basic emotional needs of their children by showing unconditional love. The statistics show we parents are failing to do this.

It is a fact, though, that most parents do love their children. Again, the basic problem is that we are not aware that we *must* convey our love to our children *before anything else:* before teaching, before guidance, before example, before discipline. Unconditional love must be the basic relationship with a child, or everything else is unpredictable, especially their attitudes and behavior.

But we should not be pessimistic about this. The really encouraging thing is that we know what the basic problem is and we know how to combat it. There are reasonable answers. I am convinced that most parents, because they love their child, can be *taught* to convey this love to him. The difficult question is, how can we get this across to all (or at least most) parents? This is something which all concerned parents must consider. The answer will require the input and action of many.

6

How to Love Your Child —Focused Attention

Eye contact and physical contact seldom require real sacrifice by parents. Focused attention does, however, require time, and sometimes a lot of it. It may mean giving up something parents would rather do. Loving parents will see times when a child desperately needs focused attention at a time when the parents feel least like giving it.

What is focused attention? Focused attention is giving a child our full, undivided attention in such a way that he feels without doubt that he is completely loved. That he is valuable enough *in his own right* to warrant parents' undistracted watchfulness, appreciation, and uncompromising regard. In short, focused attention makes a child feel he is the most important person in the world in his parents' eyes.

Some may think this is going a bit too far, but take a look at Scripture and see how highly children are regarded. Notice the high priority Christ gave them (Mark 10:13-16). Their value is stressed in the Psalms (Ps. 127:3-5), and in Genesis, children are referred to as gifts (Gen. 33:5).

A child ought to be made to feel he is the only one of his kind. Few children feel this but oh, the difference it makes in that small one when he knows he is special. Only focused attention can give him that realization and knowledge. It is so vital in a child's development of self-esteem. And it profoundly affects a child's ability to relate to and love others.

Focused attention, in my experience, is the most demanding need a child has, because we parents have extreme difficulty in recognizing it, much less fulfilling it. There are many reasons we do not recognize this particular need. One of the main reasons is that other things we do for a child seem to suffice. For example, special favors (ice cream or candy), gifts, and granting unusual requests seem to substitute for focused attention at the time. These kindnesses are good, but it is a serious mistake to use them as a stand-in for genuine focused attention. I find it a real temptation to use this type of substitution because favors or gifts are easier to give and take much less of my time. But I have found over and and over again that my children do not do their best, do not feel their best, and do not behave their best unless I give them that precious commodity, focused attention.

The Tyranny of the Urgent

Why is it so difficult to give focused attention? Because it takes *time*. Numerous studies have been done and books written showing that time is our most precious possession. Put it this way. Given 24 hours a day, seven days a week, it is virtually impossible to fulfill all of our obligations. That is a true statement and forces me to stop and think. It is not possible for me to take care of every obligation and every responsibility in my life as I would like it to be done. I *must* face up to that fact. If I do not, I will naively assume that everything will somehow get taken care of, and, when I assume that, I will become controlled by the tyranny of the urgent. Urgent matters will then automatically take precedence in my life and control my time. This would be fine if these urgent matters were important matters. Unfortunately they usually are not. Take the sacred telephone, for example. I say sacred because it takes precedence over almost all else. The ringing telephone must be answered regardless of time, place, or situation. Our family may be having a few wonderful moments together at supper time. This is of the highest importance to me. But if the urgent telephone rings, it is given almost sacred right to interfere with, disrupt, and even destroy our family fellowship. The tyranny of the urgent wins out over the important things of life once again.

You know, there is just not enough time in our short lives to be controlled by the urgent and be able to look after the important. We can't have our cake and eat it too. So what can we do about it? I'm afraid there is only one answer. And it isn't simple or easy. We must determine our priorities, set our goals, and plan our time to accomplish them. *We* must control our time in order to take care of the important things.

Set Priorities

What are the priorities in your life? Where does your child fit in? Does he take first priority? Second? Third? Fourth? You must determine this! Otherwise, your child will take a low precedence and suffer from some degree of neglect.

No one else can do this for you. A spouse cannot set his own or your child's priority in *your* life. Nor can your minister, counselor, employer, or friend. Only you can do this. So what is it, fellow parent? What and who gets priority in your life?—Job? Church? Spouse? House? Hobby? Children? Television? Social life? Career?

Please let me refer again to my personal experience and to those of my counselees. Thus far in my adventure of living, I have noticed the following. In almost all families that have found contentment, satisfaction, happiness, and genuine thankfulness among all family members, the parents possess a similar priority system. Usually their first priority is of an ethical nature, such as a strong religious faith or moral code. In most cases, this is manifested by placing God first in their lives and having a warm, comforting, loving, supportive relationship with Him. They use this stabilizing relationship to influence all other relationships. Their second priority is the spouse, as discussed previously. The children take priority number three. As you can see, real happiness is found in family orientation—spiritual family then physical family. God, spouse, children. These are essential. The remaining priorities are important, of course, but these three must come first.

I have talked to many people who sought contentment in such things as money, power, and prestige. But as they experienced life and discovered real values, they sadly realized they were investing in the wrong account. I've seen numerous wealthy persons who spent their better years making it. Tragically, they had to seek counseling when they realized that, despite their wealth and power, their lives were pathetically and painfully empty. Each would weep and consider his life a "failure" because of a wayward child or a spouse lost through divorce. They realize only then that the only worthwhile possession in life is someone who loves you and cares what happens to you—God, spouse, and child.

I've also seen many persons who are terminally ill, and their most profound realization in life is exactly the same. As they look back on life, they too know that the only thing that really matters is whether someone genuinely cares for and unconditionally loves them. If these persons do have such loved ones, they are content. If they do not, they are to be pitied.

I recently talked with the wife of a minister, a most beautiful woman who has incurable cancer. She is such a radiant wholesome person. As we talked, she explained how, since she has known of her illness, her outlook on life has been transformed. With the knowledge of impending death, her priority system was forced to change. For the first time she realized there was not enough time in the life of *any* parent to provide for the needs of spouse and children if less important things were not resisted. This minister's wife gave her husband and children first priority, and what a difference was evident in their lives. More wonderfully changed husband and children I've never seen. Of course, this does not mean we should neglect other areas of our lives, but we must control the time we spend on them and their influence on us.

Fleeting Moments
This illustration poignantly points out the importance of focused

attention. I recently read of a father who was sitting in his living room one day. It was his fiftieth birthday, and he happened to be in an irritable mood. Suddenly his 11 year-old-boy Rick bounced into the room, sat on his father's lap and began kissing him repeatedly on the cheeks. The boy continued his kissing until his father sharply asked, "What are you doing?" The child answered, "I'm giving you 50 kisses on your fiftieth birthday." Ordinarily the father would have been touched by this loving act of affection. Unfortunately, because he was depressed and irritable, he pushed the boy away and stated, "Let's do that some other time." The boy was crushed. He ran out of the house, jumped on his bike and rode away. A few moments later the child was struck and killed by a car. You can imagine the grief, remorse, and guilt suffered by this poor father.

These stories tell us several things. First, because life is so unpredictable and uncertain, we cannot know or plan how many opportunities will be allowed us for nurturing our children. Especially, how many moments we will have to give focused attention. We must take advantage of our timely opportunities because they are fewer than we may realize. Our children are growing up.

Secondly, these moments of opportunity do not happen every day. Remember those special moments which leave a lasting impression on a child? That moment when Rick tried to kiss his father 50 times was one such priceless moment. If the father had been able to spend those few moments with Rick in a positive way, Rick would have affectionately remembered that time the rest of his life, especially when tempted to act against parental values, as, for example, in the dissident days of adolescence. However, if Rick had not been killed, he would never have forgotten the pain, anguish, and humiliation of that moment.

Let's look at another story regarding focused attention. In the diary of the father of a great humanitarian was found a description of a day spent fishing with his son. The father laments how the day was a "total loss" because the son seemed "bored and preoccupied, saying very little." The father even wrote that he probably would not take his son fishing again.

Many years later a historian found these notes, and with curiosity compared them with the entries of the same day in the son's diary. The son exclaimed what a "perfect day" it had been, "all alone" with his father. He described how deeply meaningful and important it was to him.

The Goal of Focused Attention

What is it that defines focused attention? When a child feels, "I'm all alone with my mommy (or daddy)"; "I have her (him) all to myself"; "at this moment, I'm the most important person in the world to my mother (father)"; this is the goal of focused attention, to enable a child to feel this way.

Focused attention is not something that is nice to give our child if time permits, it is a critical *need* each child has. How a child views himself and how he is accepted by his world is determined by the way in which this need is met. Without focused attention, a child experiences increased anxiety because he feels everything else is more important than he. A child is consequently less secure and is impaired in his emotional and psychological growth. Such a child can be identified in the nursery or classroom. He is less mature than children whose parents have taken the time to fill their need for focused attention. This unfortunate child is generally more withdrawn and has difficulty with peers. He is less able to cope and usually reacts poorly in any conflict. He is overly dependent upon the teacher or other adults he comes into contact with.

Some children, especially girls deprived of focused attention from their fathers, *seem* to be just the opposite. They are quite talkative, manipulative, dramatic, often childishly seductive, and are usually considered precocious, outgoing, and mature by their kindergarten and first grade teachers. However, as they grow older, this behavior pattern does not change and becomes gradually inappropriate. By the time they are in the third or fourth grade they are usually obnoxious to their peers, and to their teachers. However, even at this late date, focused attention, especially from the fathers, can go a long way in reducing the children's self-defeating behavior, decreasing their anxiety, and freeing them to resume their maturational growth.

How to Give Focused Attention

Now that we've seen how vital focused attention is to a child, how do we accomplish it? I have found that the best way to give a child focused attention is to set aside time to spend with him *alone*. I'll bet you're already thinking how difficult it is to do this. You are right. Finding time to be alone with a child, free from other distractions, is what I consider to be the most difficult aspect of good child rearing. You might say this separates the best parents from other parents. The sacrificing parents from the nonsacrificing; the most caring from the least caring; the parents who set priorities from those who do not. Let's face it, good child rearing takes *time*. Finding time in our hyperactive society is hard, especially when children often are addicted to television and sometimes would rather spend time with it. This is all the more reason focused attention is so crucial. Children are being influenced by forces outside the family more than anytime in history. It takes tremendous effort to pry time from busy schedules, but the rewards are great. It is a wonderful thing to see your child happy, secure, well liked by peers and adults, and learning and behaving at his best. But believe me, fellow parent, this does not come automatically. We must pay a price for it! We must find time to spend alone with each child.

John Alexander, President of Inter-Varsity Christian Fellowship, has four children. At a recent conference, he was relating how difficult it was for him to find time for each of them. His solution was to save at least one-half hour every Sunday afternoon for each of his children. Everyone must find his own way of doing this.

My time is also difficult to manage. I try to conserve it as much as possible for my children. For example, at one time my daughter was taking lessons close to my office Monday afternoons. I would schedule my appointments so that I could pick her up myself. Then we would stop at a restaurant and have supper together. At these times, without the pressure of interruption and time schedules, I was able to give her my full attention and listen to whatever she wanted to talk about. Only in this context of being alone without pressure can parents and their child develop that special indelible relationship which each child so desperately needs to face the realities of life. It's such moments as these that a child remembers when life becomes difficult, especially during those tumultuous years of adolescent conflict and the normal drives for independence.

It's also during times of focused attention that parents can take special opportunities to make eye contact and physical contact with a child. It is during times of focused attention that eye and physical contact have stronger meaning and impact upon a child's life.

Of course, it is more difficult to find time for focused attention as one has more children. I remember counseling a seven-year-old girl for numerous problems she was having at school and at home. Problems with school work, peer relationships, sibling relationships, and immature behavior. You've perhaps guessed the problem already. She had nine brothers and sisters and her dear parents couldn't find the time to give her the focused attention she needed. Actually, they weren't aware that this girl was suffering from lack of focused attention because all their other children were quite well adjusted. The parents were farmers and during the natural course of a day—milking, feeding the animals, and plowing—they spent sufficient time alone with each child to forestall problems. With this particular child, because of her age, individual chores, and birth order, the natural course of events prevented her from enjoying enough of her parents' attention. She felt neglected and unloved. Her parents loved her dearly but the child did not feel it and so did not know it.

Careful Planning Pays Off

We see from this illustration how important it is to *plan* our time in order to provide focused attention for *each* child. This is difficult. In a two-child family, each parent is often able to spend time with one of the children. With more than two children, the problem becomes progressively more difficult. And, of course, in a one-parent family the logistics are more difficult. However careful planning pays off: for example, on a particular day, (say next Friday), one child may be invited to a party, another may be at a relative's, leaving one child free. A careful parent whose children take priority would consider this time a golden opportunity to give focused attention to that child. Of course, our plans must consider the emotional needs of each and every child or we'll have the same problem as in the 10-child family we just discussed. This is especially difficult when we have both a demanding and a nondemanding child in the same family. We must resist the concept that the loudest hinge gets the oil. Every child has the same needs whether he demands they be met or not. Especially vulnerable in this regard is a non-demanding, passive child who also is a middle child. And if his siblings happen to be demanding children, his parents will find it all too easy to pass him by until problems develop.

Watching for unexpected opportunities yields additional time. For example, times occur when a parent just finds himself alone with a child, as when the others are outside playing. Here is another opportunity to fill that child's emotional tank and prevent problems brought on by a dry one. This time of focused attention may be quite short, just a moment or two can do wonders. Every moment counts. It's like making deposits in a savings account. As long as the balance is healthy, a child's emotional life will be sound and he will have fewer problems. It's also an investment in the future, especially the years of adolescence.

Every deposit is assurance that a child's teenage years will be healthy, wholesome, pleasant, and rewarding for both child and parent. The stakes are high. What's worse than a wayward adolescent son or daughter? What's more wonderful than a well-balanced teenager?

Of course, longer periods of focused attention are important also. As children grow older, this time of focus needs to be lengthened. Older children need time to warm up, let their developing defenses down, and feel free to share their innermost thoughts, especially anything that may be troubling them. As you can see, if these times of focused attention were begun early in a child's life, he accepts it very naturally and finds it much easier to share emotional things with his parents. On the other hand, if times for focused attention are not provided, how can a child learn to communicate meaningfully with his parents? Again, the stakes are high. What is worse than having a troubled child who can't share his feelings with you? What is more wonderful than for your child to be able to bring anything to you to talk over?

All this is difficult and takes time. But many people I've met have shared with me all sorts of ways they have done this. I remember listening to Joe Bayly, a Christian writer, who was talking about this. He marks off definite times on his appointment calendar to spend with his family, and when someone calls and asks him to accept a speaking engagement at that time, he politely tells the inquirer that he has another engagement.

Another idea I particularly liked from Joe Bayly was the use of personal flags, one for each family member. Each flag would be designed to suit the personality of that particular member, with his name visible on it. It was usually given to a child on his birthday. Thereafter it was flown on the flag pole in front of the house on special occasions, for example, subsequent birthdays, when that child would return home after trips, or going away to college. This is an example of indirect focused attention.

When Others Are Present

We mentioned that focused attention is given when alone with a child, away from other family members. Although this is true, there are times when focused attention must be given with others present. This is especially true when a child is ill, has experienced some emotional pain, or for some other painful reason has regressed. By regressed, I mean he is in poor control of his feelings and/or behavior.

Let me give you an example of this. One day, deeply concerned parents sought my advice regarding their 12-year-old son Tim. The boy's first cousin, also a 12-year-old boy had come to live with them. The cousin was a very demanding child who had overshadowed Tim by taking almost all his parents' attention. Tim felt displaced by his overpowering cousin, became depressed, withdrawn, and occasionally uncommunicative. Part of my advice to the parents was, of course, to give both Tim and his cousin much focused attention, that is, spend time with Tim alone and the cousin, alone. However, the cousin continued to clearly dominate each situation when the two boys were present. Next, I advised the parents to give each boy focused attention whenever the cousin was being overly dominant. The parents were able to do this by turning directly toward Tim when it was his turn to speak, giving him full eye contact, and physical contact when convenient, and responding to his comments. Then when it was appropriately Tim's cousin's turn to speak, the parents repeated the process with him.

This type of focused attention usually works well only if a child is also receiving ample focused attention alone. By the way, I've taught teachers these simple principles which have revolutionized their teaching and perceptions toward each child.

Focused attention is time consuming, difficult to do consistently, and many times burdensome to already exhausted parents. But focused attention is the most powerful means of keeping a child's emotional tank full and investing in his future.

7

Appropriate
and Inappropriate Love

I'd like to consider the *too much love* controversy. One side of the argument states that too much love will spoil the child, while the other side claims that you can't love a child too much. The confusion in this area often causes advocates of both sides to take extreme positions. Many of the former group, for example, are severe disciplinarians while many of the latter group are over-indulgent.

I would like to invite you to re-examine the issue in light of the concept of *appropriate love*. I believe that if we define appropriate love as that love which, when conveyed to a child, will provide healthy nurturing and foster a child's emotional growth and self-reliance, then the picture will become clear. We can then hold to the principle that a child needs a superabundance of appropriate love and, of course, a child needs no inappropriate love.

Inappropriate Love
I believe we may define *inappropriate love* as affection which, when conveyed to a child, hinders a child's emotional growth by failing to meet a child's emotional needs, and which fosters an increasingly dependent relationship upon a parent and hampers self-reliance.

The four most common types of inappropriate love are possessiveness, seductiveness, vicariousness, and role-reversal. Let's take them one at a time.

Possessiveness

Possessiveness is a tendency of parents to encourage a child to be too dependent on his parents. Paul Tournier, famed Swiss counselor, deals with the subject quite well in his article, "The Meaning of Possessiveness." He states that when a child is small, dependency is "obvious and almost complete." But if this dependence does not diminish as a child grows older, it becomes an obstacle to a child's emotional development. Many parents try to keep their children in a state of dependence upon them. Dr. Tournier states that they do this "by suggestion or by emotional blackmail," or else by using their authority and insisting upon obedience. The child is theirs. They have rights over him because he belongs to them. Such parents are termed *possessive*. These parents tend to treat their child as an object or property to be possessed or owned, and not as a person who needs to grow in his own right and to become gradually independent and self-reliant.

A child must have respect from his parents to be himself. This does not, of course, mean no limit-setting or being permissive. (Every child needs guidance and discipline.) It means to encourage a child to think, to be spontaneous, to realize he is a separate person who must assume more and more responsibility for himself.

If we parents disregard a child's right to gradually become independent, one of two things will happen. He may become overly dependent on us and overly submissive, failing to learn how to live in his world. He may become easy prey to strong-willed, authoritative personalities or groups such as the Moonies; or there will be deterioration of our relationship with a child as he gets older. He will become more resistant to our guidance.

Again, as Dr. Tournier suggests, we should "possess as if not possessing. Such is the great message of the Bible. Man can never truly possess anything. He is but the steward of the goods that God entrusts to him, for "the earth is the Lord's, and everything in it" (1 Cor. 10:26, NIV).

Of course there is some possessiveness in every parent. But we must take care to (1) identify it within ourselves, (2) separate it from true concern for a child's total welfare, especially concerning his need to become self-reliant, (3) be as continuously aware of it as we can, (4) resist its influence.

Seductiveness

The second inappropriate way of expressing love is through seductiveness. I have to start out by saying this is a difficult subject to write about because *seductiveness* is not easy to define. The word seems to be used to communicate everything from elicitation of sexual experience to pollution.

Regarding our subject at hand, I believe it sufficient to define seductiveness as attempting consciously or unconsciously to derive sensual/sexual feelings from an encounter with a child.

An example of this was discussed at a recent seminar on child psychiatry. A seven-year-old girl was seen at a psychiatric clinic for frequent masturbation and poor school performance. The evaluation disclosed that the child spent much time fantasizing (daydreaming) her mother's death and living alone with her father. It was also noted that her father spent much time holding the child, caressing and fondling her in such a way that seemed to bring sensual enjoyment to both father and child. When these facts were gently shared with the father, his response was, "Oh, my word! I just realized that when I wash the soap off of her when we're showering together, she reacts like a mature woman." This was a case where the father was obviously seductive. However, he apparently did not (fully) realize what he was doing. As in almost all cases of this sort, the marital relationship in this family was hurting. In families where the marriage is not healthy it is not uncommon for seductiveness to exist, although usually not to this degree.

What do you think of this letter to Ann Landers which appeared in her syndicated column on December 28, 1976?

"Dear Ann Landers: I don't know if I have a problem or not. It's our beautiful 12-year-old daughter. I've seen girls who are crazy about their fathers, but never anything quite like this.

"Donna sits next to (or on top of) him at every opportunity. They play with each others hands and act kittenish like a couple of goofy kids. She hangs on her father when they walk or their arms are around one another's waists. Is this normal? Signed, Me Worried."

Are you a parent of a preadolescent daughter? What do you think? Does this sound good or bad? Would you be worried? What would you do?

Let's look at Ann Landers' reply:

"Dear W: Sounds to me as if there's entirely too much touching. Today a girl of 12 is more of a woman than a child. Donna needs to be talked to, but it would be better if the word did not come from you.

"Perhaps an enlightened relative or an adult friend could tell Donna it is unbecoming and unhealthy for a young girl to have so much physical contact with her father. (Surely this behavior has been observed by others.)

"If you know of no person you might call on to communicate the message tactfully but firmly, by all means enlist the help of the school counselor. I believe Donna should be approached rather than your husband. He is apt to be resentful and defensive."

I would like to reply to Ann's reply. First, I agree that it does sound like there is too much physical contact here, and it does sound seductive. However, this is the mother's viewpoint and the chances are overwhelming that the marital relationship is poor. In short, neither we (nor Ann) know for sure if there is actually sensual seduction here or not. Perhaps this situation is similar to the one at the end of chapter 2 where the mother is jealous of a good relationship between daughter and father.

Supposing the relationship here is indeed a seductive one, would you go to a 12-year-old girl and suggest that her own father was sexually improper with her? Genuine respect for parents is hard enough to find today without further undermining it.

But nonetheless there is one principal comment I'd like to make regarding Ann's reply and that is that it exemplifies the general mentality today regarding loving children. Her advice was that, because the father was conveying his love to the child inappropriately, he should not show it at all. We have already seen how vital physical contact is to a preadolescent girl. This particular father was not doing it correctly. Is the answer to stop the physical contact completely?

I'm afraid this type of reaction has become generally accepted by our society. It is generally assumed that because some parents are seductive with their children, physical contact should be held to a minimum or actually be avoided. An analogy would be this: because I saw an obese person today, I should not eat at all, or at least minimally.

Another reason many parents unfortunately avoid physical contact with their children is that they may actually feel some sexual response to them. This can happen to any parents, especially fathers of older daughters. So this is indeed a dilemma. On the one hand, the child desperately needs to feel loved and physical contact is essential for this. On the other hand, the parents feel uncomfortable and fear this would be wrong or perhaps damaging to the child.

I think many loving parents would be greatly helped in this difficult area if they realized that: (1) every child regardless of age needs *appropriate* physical contact, (2) to have some occasional sexual feelings or fleeting sexual fantasies regarding a child is normal, (3) a parent should ignore these inappropriate feelings, go ahead, and give a child what he (or she) needs, including appropriate (nonseductive) physical contact.

With this confusion is it any wonder so few children feel genuinely, unconditionally loved?

Another fear many parents have regarding seductiveness is homosexuality. There seems to be a misconception that too much love expressed from mother to daughter or from father to son will lead to homosexuality, but just the opposite is the case.

It's not infrequent during my work in schools for a teacher to approach me with this concern. A woman teacher recently asked, "Dr. Campbell, I love my daughter so very much that I kiss her a lot and sometimes on the lips. Am I making a lesbian out of her?" After asking for other information to make sure the relationship was healthy, my answer was, "Keep it up."

Two Examples

Let me give you two other examples. The second example will show what appropriate love, including physical contact, does for a child concerning sexual identity. But the first example concerns what the *absence* of it *causes*.

The first example is drawn from Rusty, a very dear friend of mine who is mean, tough, "all man," and a drill instructor in the U.S. Marine Corps. He and his wonderfully warm sensitive wife have four boys, "stair steps." Rusty decided his boys were going to be like him, tough and rugged men. He treated them like Marine recruits with strict and rigid discipline, no affection, unquestioned obedience, and no questions.

Your reaction to this is important. How do you think these boys developed? Do you think they are following in their father's footsteps? Do you think they're becoming "all men"?

The last time I saw these boys each one was extremely effeminate. Their mannerisms, speech, and appearance were those of girls. Surprised? You shouldn't be. I see it every day. Boys with rejecting, harsh, non-affectionate fathers generally become effeminate.

Here's the second example. Several years ago we had a pastor who was a huge man with rugged features. His very presence demanded attention, and he had a warm, loving heart. His boy at that time was three years old, the same age as my David but a head taller and about twenty pounds heavier, a "spittin' image of his ol' man." Our pastor loved his son deeply and warmly. He was very affectionate with the boy, lots of holding, hugging, kissing, and wrestling.

How do you think this boy developed? Did he follow in his father's footsteps? You bet he did. That little fellow was just like his father. He had a strong, healthy sexual identification and was secure, happy, lovable, and all boy. He will do all right in this world with a dad like that.

If these two examples don't convince you that a superabundance of appropriate love is not only warranted, but needed by every child (girls *and* boys) from *each* parent, let me give you this one fact. In all my reading and experience, I have never known of one sexually disoriented person who had a warm, loving, and affectionate father.

So, due to these misconceptions we've just looked at (and others), few parents are able to properly nourish their children emotionally. Although there is abundant love in their hearts, there is little in their practice. I am convinced that once these misconceptions are corrected, and once parents understand what a child needs, most are able to provide the superabundance of appropriate love each child must have.

Vicariousness

The third most common type of inappropriate love is vicariousness. *Vicariousness,* or vicarious love, is living one's life or dreams through the life of a child. One of the most harmful kinds of vicariousness is a mother's living out romantic fantasies or longings through her daughter. A mother does this by steering her daughter into relationships and situations where she herself longs to be. A clue to this phenomenon is a mother's obsessive interests in the intimate details of her child's dating experiences, becoming sensually excited as her daughter reveals them to her. The destructiveness of this process is obvious. A child can be led into situations which she does not have the maturity or experience to handle. Pregnancy is just one possible consequence. Another frequent outgrowth of this is a degrading reputation for the child. Such a reputation can injure a child's self-image and self-respect for life.

This type of vicariousness can also happen between father and son with similar consequences. A father who acts out his own sexual prowess through his son's conquests is harming not only his son but others involved in his life. In this way the boy is heavily influenced to view women primarily as sexual objects. He will find it difficult to relate to women as persons with feelings, and especially as equals.

Of course there are many varieties of vicariousness. The kind just described happens to be the most destructive.

Another example of vicariousness is a father using his son to satisfy athletic longings of his own. If you would like to see this phenomenon in action, go to your nearest Little League game. A vicariously-oriented parent becomes emotionally involved in the game to such an extent it is as though he himself were the player. You can see him becoming outrageously angry at the umpire when the call is against his son. Worst of all such a parent will reprimand and demean his son when he makes a mistake.

What does this bring to mind? The old problem of conditional love. The more vicarious we are with our children, the more our love for them is conditional upon how well they have performed and have met our own vicarious needs.

But let's face it. We're all vicarious to some extent, aren't we? Last summer we discovered that our eight-year-old son is a pretty good baseball player. As I sat there watching him play, for some strange reason my mind drifted back to my professional baseball days. I would find myself recalling how desperately I wanted to make it to the major leagues. The pain and disappointment of failing to accomplish this focused before me as I watched David doing so well. I wonder why. What a mistake it will be if I vicariously attempt to fulfill my lost dream through my son. I'd better watch myself.

Vicariousness becomes harmful when it modifies our love so that it is given in relation to a child's behavior and is, in fact, conditional love. We parents must not let our own hopes, longings, and dreams determine the type of love a child receives.

Vicariousness can be considered a kind of possessiveness if it causes us to view children as possessions to be used to fulfill our own dream. How can a child grow in his own right and think for himself and rely on himself in this situation?

We must keep our love for a child unconditional. We must love him so that he can fulfill God's plan for his life, not our vicarious ones.

Role-Reversal

Role-reversal was described by M.A. Morris and R.W. Gould in their Child Welfare League publication in 1963. They define this "as a reversal of the dependency role, in which parents turn to their infants and small children for nurturing and protection."

Brandt Steele and Carl Pollock present a description of role-reversal in the book, *The Battered Child*, (Chicago: University of Chicago Press, 1974 p. 95). They state: "These parents expect and demand a great deal from their infants and children. Not only is the demand for performance great, but it is premature, clearly beyond the ability of the infant to comprehend what is wanted and to respond appropriately. [These] Parents deal with the child as if he were much older than he really is. Observation of this interaction leads to a clear impression that the parent feels insecure and unsure of being loved, and looks to the child as a source of reassurance, comfort, and loving response. It is hardly an exaggeration to say the parent acts like a frightened, unloved child, looking to his own child as if he were an adult capable of providing comfort and love. . . . We see two basic elements involved—a high expectation and demand by the parent for the child's performance and a corresponding parental disregard of the infant's own needs, limited abilities, and helplessness—a significant misperception of the infant by the parent."

Role-reversal is the primary relationship in the frightening phenomenon of child abuse. An abusing parent feels his child must take care of the parent's emotional needs, that the parent has a right to be comforted and nourished by his child. When the child fails in this, the parent feels a right to punish him.

Child abuse is the extreme form of role-reversal, but all parents use role-reversal to some extent. Sometimes we expect our child to make us feel better. These times usually occur when we ourselves are not feeling well, either physically or mentally. We may be depressed, physically ill, mentally or physically exhausted. At these times we have little or no emotional nurturing to provide our child. It can then be very difficult to give him eye contact, physical contact, or focused attention. When our emotional or physical resources are drained, we need nurturing ourselves. It's difficult to give when we have little or nothing to give. In this condition it's so easy to make the mistake of expecting our child to be comforting, reassuring, compliant, mature in his behavior, and passively obedient. These are not the characteristics of a normal child. If made to assume this unhealthy role, a child will not develop normally. The list of possible disturbances which can result is endless.

We parents must not allow such a situation to develop. We must understand that parents do the nurturing, and a child receives it. During times when we are unable to carry this out, we must recuperate as quickly as possible. And until we are ready to resume this crucial parental responsibility, we must not look to our children to parent us. Of course they can help us as they are able, running errands and getting things for us when we're sick, but they must not be expected to nurture us emotionally.

We should make every attempt to prevent such times when we are unable to nurture our children. This may mean better care of our bodies to prevent illness and fatigue, for example, a sensible diet, plenty of rest, and plenty of exercise. It may mean looking out for our emotional health by engaging in hobbies or other refreshing activities to prevent depression or mental exhaustion. It may mean keeping our spiritual life fresh and exciting by allowing ample time for prayer and meditation. Most importantly, it means keeping our marriages strong, healthy, and secure. Wife or husband must take second priority and our children a close third. Remember, we will be able to give more to our child if we keep ourselves emotionally and spiritually replenished. This gets back to setting priorities and planning toward goals.

Don't Throw Out the Baby with the Bath Water
We have looked at the four most common types of inappropriate

love and several common misconceptions. Of course, these are ways of relating which we want to avoid. They are good neither for the child nor the parent.

However, as we avoid these mistakes, let's not "throw out the baby with the bath water." Let's not make a worse mistake and withhold *appropriate* love from our child. This is the most common of all child rearing mistakes. Far more children suffer from the lack of appropriate love than from exposure to inappropriate love.

Appropriate love is for the benefit and welfare of the child. Inappropriate love serves the abnormal needs and hang-ups of the parent.

We must face it. Our children have essential needs which only parents can fill. If we find we cannot fill these needs, if we cannot keep their emotional tanks full, if we can't give them an abundance of eye contact, physical contact, and focused attention appropriately, we had better get help, and fast. The longer we wait, the worse the situation will become.

8

Discipline:
What Is It?

Periodically, I give a lecture series on parent-child relationships for churches and civic groups. I cover the material in a manner similar to this book. We spend three or four hours talking about how to love a child before we deal with discipline. Invariably, after two or three hours, a parent will come up to me and say, "I've enjoyed the lectures so far, but when do we get to discipline? That's where I have problems and need answers."

This poor parent has usually misunderstood (1) the relationship between love and discipline, and (2) the meaning of discipline. He has separated love from discipline in his mind as though they are two separate entities. No wonder this parent is confused and has problems controlling his child.

Parents who are confused in this way have usually assumed that discipline means punishment (chastisement according to some).

Both of these assumptions are false. I stress to those parents and I hope to stress to you, fellow parent, that love and discipline cannot be separated, and that punishment is a very small part of discipline.

The first fact we must understand in order to have a well-disciplined child is that *making a child feel loved is the first and most important part of good discipline.* Of course this is not all, but it is most important.

What has been mentioned thus far in this book is the most important aspect of discipline, and must be applied if we can expect the best results from disciplining our child. There is no point in reading further at this time if you have not applied what you have already read, and if you have not kept your child's emotional tank full. If you have not made your child feel loved with an abundance of eye contact, physical contact, and focused attention in an appropriate way, *please do not read further.* The results will disappoint you. Application of behavioral control techniques without a foundation of unconditional love is barbaric and unscriptural. You may have a child who is well-behaved when he is young, but the results are most discouraging in the long run. Only a healthy love-bond relationship lasts through all of life's crises.

What Is Discipline?
Before we go on we should look at a definition of discipline. What is it? In the realm of child rearing, discipline is *training* a child in mind and character to enable him to become a self-controlled, constructive member of society. What does this involve? Discipline involves training through every type of communication. Guidance by example, modeling, verbal instruction, written instruction, verbal requests, written requests, teaching, providing learning and fun experiences. The list is quite long.

Yes, punishment is on this list, but it is only one of many ways of discipline and is the most negative and primitive factor. Unfortunately we must use it at times and we will discuss its use further. At present, it should be reemphasized that guidance toward right thought and action is far superior to punishment for wrong action.

With a clear definition of discipline in mind, consider it again in relation to unconditional love. *Discipline is immeasurably easier when the child feels genuinely loved.* This is because he wants to identify with the parents, and is able to do so only if he knows he is truly loved and accepted. He is then able to accept his parents' guidance without hostility and obstructiveness.

If a child does not feel genuinely loved and accepted, however, he has real difficulty identifying with his parents *and* their values. Without a strong, healthy love-bond with his parents, a child reacts to parental guidance with anger, hostility and resentment. He views each parental request (or command) as an imposition and learns to resist it. In severe cases, a child learns to consider each parental request with such resentment that his total orientation to parental (and eventually to all) authority is one of doing exactly the opposite of what is expected of him. This type of emotional disorder is increasing at an alarming rate in our country, and children from Christian families are not excluded.

I hope you are realizing how crucial unconditional love is for good discipline (training). The more we keep a child's emotional tank full, the more he will respond to discipline (training). The less full his emotional tank, the less he will respond to discipline (training).

One aspect of appropriate love not yet mentioned is focused (active) listening. Focused listening is listening to a child in such a way that he is sure you know what he is trying to communicate to you. When a child knows that you understand how he feels and what he wants, he is much more willing to respond positively to discipline, especially when you disagree with him. Nothing frustrates a child more than to be told to do something when he feels his parents don't understand his position. This does not mean catering to a child's demand or whim, it simply means listening to a child so that he doesn't feel you have ignored his thoughts and feelings when you use your authority. Is that unreasonable? If you believe it is, you are not regarding your child as a valuable, separate person.

Think about it. When your child feels you have considered his position and feelings, you have assuaged anger and resentment which could come back to haunt you later. Doesn't your heavenly Father do as much for you? Christ said, "Ask and you will be given what you ask for. Seek, and you will find. Knock, and the door will be opened. For everyone who asks, receives. Anyone who seeks, finds. If only you will knock, the door will open. If a child asks his father for a loaf of bread, will he be given a stone instead? If he asks for fish, will he be given a poisonous snake? Of course not! And if you hardhearted, sinful men know how to give good gifts to your children, won't your Father in heaven even more certainly give good gifts to those who ask Him for them?" (Matt. 7:7-11, LB)

To give a child focused listening requires at least eye contact, with physical contact and focused attention if possible and if appropriate. Acknowledging that you understand a child (even if you disagree with him) is usually helpful. Repeating a child's thoughts and feelings back to him is a good way to ensure that he understands that you understand. A child's thoughts and feelings may make a difference in your own understanding and actions also.

I recall an incident with my 16-year-old daughter. It's not hard to recall because it happened recently. We let her go to a wrestling match at her high school on a school night with three other kids. She was told to come home right after the match. The match was to end around 10 o'clock. It usually takes 30 to 45 minutes to make the trip. At 11 o'clock I became concerned; at 11:15 I called the parents of one of the boys. They said the group had stopped by there to get a car with snow tires (bad weather had begun) and the parents decided to offer them a snack. The kids had left the home about 11:10. My daughter arrived home at 11:40.

I was angry. I sent her to bed after giving her a lecture about responsibility, and placed her on one week's restriction (she was grounded). Why did I react without listening to what the child had to say? I was thinking more of myself than the actual situation. I wasn't feeling well that night and wanted to get to bed early. I had a very busy schedule the next day. Secondly, my daughter was later than I expected and she did not call to tell us that she would be late. I assumed she was totally negligent in the whole situation.

I have a wise daughter. She waited until the next day when I had recovered my composure and loving ways before giving me all the facts. She also knew that I listen better (focused listening) when I am not angry. As it turned out the kids took the safe way home, which is longer. Ice and snow were making the roads slippery. She was telling the truth, it all checked. Where she had been negligent was failing to call us when she saw that she would be later than we expected. After apologizing to her for overreacting, I decreased the restriction to be commensurate with what she had done.

There are two lessons we can learn from this experience. The first is the importance of really listening to a child when he is communicating. I could have saved myself frustration and my daughter's pain and possible anger and resentment toward me by listening to her before acting.

The other lesson is the importance of controlling our emotions at such times. I do believe that a parent's worst enemy in raising his child is his own uncontrolled feelings, especially anger. As in the experience just described, this can cause us to say or do things we will regret later. Too much anger, especially uncontrolled anger, will frighten a child initially. It may even seem to help a child's behavior, but this is only temporary. As a child grows older, parental expression of too much anger (temper outbursts), will instill increased disrespect for the parents along with kindling a child's own anger and gradual resentment. When you stop to think about it, uncontrolled feelings draw disrespect from anyone. Why should we expect otherwise from our spouse or child?

You know as well as I that we all lose our cool at times. One thing to remember is that when we do, we shouldn't be afraid to apologize later after things have calmed down. It's very possible to make a beautiful thing out of a bad one. It's amazing how pleasant communications can become when a family member is big enough to apologize when he is wrong, and losing one's calm inappropriately (overreacting) can be such an occasion. Believe it or not, the times of warmness and closeness that usually follow this are among those special memories that a child (and parents) never forgets. They are priceless.

Emotional overreactions, however, can only be tolerated in a family to a limited extent, especially if no apology takes place. They should be kept to a minimum. How is this accomplished?

Control your Anger

It's important to remember that anger is difficult to control under certain conditions. Some of these are (1) when a person is depressed, (2) when a person is afraid, (3) when a person is physically not well, (4) when a person is fatigued mentally or physically, (5) when a person's spiritual life is not healthy.

A book could be written on coping with each of these problems. For now it must suffice to warn each parent to look out for himself mentally, emotionally, physically, and spiritually. Unhealthiness in any of these areas can hamper the parent-child relationship, the marital relationship, in fact, all relationships, primarily by hurting our ability to control our anger. Let's get in shape. Uncontrolled anger is detrimental to good discipline.

Discipline and Punishment

I hope you are realizing that we have much to do before we can expect our child to respond well to discipline. Anyone can beat a child with a rod as the primary way of controlling his behavior. That takes no sensitivity, no judgment, no understanding, and no talent. To depend on corporal punishment as the principal method of discipline is to make that critical error in assuming that discipline equals punishment. Discipline is *training* the child in the way he should go. Punishment is only one part of this, and the less the better. Please remember this statement: *the better disciplined a child is, the less punishment will be required.* How well a child responds to discipline depends primarily on how much the child feels loved and accepted. So our biggest task is to make him feel loved and accepted.

There are several reasons why so many parents fall into the punishment trap, why they somehow get the idea that their greatest responsibility in discipline (training a child) is to spank (punish) him.

One reason parents fall into this trap is because so many books, articles, seminars, institutes, radio programs, sermons, and papers advocate corporal punishment while glossing over or bypassing all other needs of a child, especially love. Few plead for a child and his real needs. Too many today are dogmatically calling for children to be punished, calling it discipline, and recommending the harshest, most extreme form of human treatment. Most perplexing of all, many of these advocates call this a biblical approach. They quote three verses from the book of Proverbs (Prov. 23:13; 29:15; 13:24) to totally justify beating a child. They neglect to mention the hundreds of Scripture verses dealing with love, compassion, sensitivity, understanding, forgiveness, nurturing, guidance, kindness, affection, and giving, as though the child has little or no right to these expressions of love.

Proponents of corporal punishment seem to have forgotten that the shepherd's rod referred to in Scripture was used almost exclusively for *guiding* the sheep, not beating them. The shepherds would *gently* steer the sheep, especially the lambs, by simply holding the rod to block them from going in the wrong direction and then gently nudge them toward the right direction. If the rod was (or is) an instrument used principally for beating, I would have a difficult time with Psalm 23 "Thy rod and Thy staff, they comfort me" (v. 4, KJV).

I have not noticed one of these advocates state that there might be times when punishment may be harmful. So many parents have come away from these gatherings or readings with the idea that corporal punishment is the primary, or even the only way to relate to a child.

The Results of this Approach

I have seen the results of this approach. Children who were passive, compliant, very quiet, withdrawn, and easily controlled when they were young, lacked a strong, healthy love-attachment to their parents, and gradually became defiant, resentful, difficult to control, self-centered, nongiving, nonaffectionate, insensitive, nonforgiving, noncompassionate, resistant to authority, and unkind as adolescents.

I think Scripture is quite helpful here. The Apostle Paul instructed, "And fathers, do not provoke your children to anger; but bring them up in the discipline and instruction of the Lord" (Eph. 6:4, NASB). What has happened to these dear children just described? Yes, they were provoked to anger by mechanical, harsh discipline (primarily punitive) without the foundation of unconditional love. I like Kenneth Taylor's paraphrase, "And now a word to you parents. Don't keep on scolding and nagging your children, making them angry and resentful. Rather, bring them up with the loving discipline the Lord himself approves, with suggestion and godly advice" (Eph. 6:4, LB).

Have you noticed that one deceptive trait of a young child who is disciplined primarily with punishment? Yes, he is easily controlled. That is the other reason so many parents fall into the trap. When a child is young, his behavior can usually be well controlled by corporal punishment alone. That is, if you consider good behavior as submissive compliance, lack of spontaneity, lack of self-confidence, and anxious docility.

You may be surprised, but I have seen many very young children who were raised with much punishment, especially corporal punishment, but who were unmanageable even at an early age. These unfortunate children would be spanked severely but the spankings would have no effect, and the children often would not even cry. Of course before coming to me, many parents have tried every piece of advice given to them from trying to give even more punishment (like pinching the trapezius muscle), to giving candy, to putting the children in certain types of rigidly structured nursery schools. In every case, one of the problems was a lack in the parent-child love bond. These children just don't feel genuinely loved and accepted. At that very early age, resentment and defiance can develop to such an extent from a lack of unconditional love that not even corporal punishment can subdue these responses.

Put the Horse before the Cart

First things first, fellow parents. Practice unconditional love, *then* discipline. Putting the horse before the cart will create a positive relationship between parents and child and will keep *negative* interactions such as corporal punishment to a minimum. Notice that I did not say unconditional love will abolish the need for corporal punishment. How I wish it could, but it won't. The more genuine and unconditional the love-bond from parents to child, the more positive is the relationship, minimizing the need for punishment. Unfortunately punishment is required at times and we'll explore that together later.

To summarize, in order for a child to respond well to discipline (training), we parents must give him what he needs. A child can learn (train) well only if he is happy, feels safe, content, confident, secure, accepted, and loved. Expecting a child to learn, namely, be disciplined, without our giving him what he needs is cruel enough. But then to beat him for not living up to our expectations? We treat our pets better than that.

Allow me to illustrate. An aggressive junior high school football coach once threatened to beat my then 13-year-old daughter with a paddle for talking while eating her lunch in the school cafeteria. I called a school official and asked him if his school system actually allowed children to be beaten (especially teenage girls by male teachers with all the sexual connotations connected with such an act). He answered "Yes!" When I asked him if he beat his dog he replied, "No." I wonder why children are becoming more and more disrespectful and resistant to authority. Can you figure it out?

The Corporal Punishment Trap

One important reason why using corporal punishment as a principal means of behavioral control is dangerous is that it drastically alleviates guilt. Corporal punishment degrades, dehumanizes, and humiliates a child. As a result, a child may feel the beating is punishment enough in itself. If the corporal punishment is instituted with enough frequency and severity, there will not be sufficient guilt provocation to enable a child to develop an adequate conscience. Without the foundation of unconditional love, the required developmental phases, especially proper parental identification, will fail to evolve, further crippling the development of a healthy conscience.

Many forget the important positive factor of guilt and consider it to be an unwanted feeling. Too much guilt is harmful but a proper amount is vital in the formation and maintenance of a normal conscience. A normal, healthy conscience which keeps a child's behavior within normal boundaries is far better than control by fear, and preferable to poor control or no control at all. What do you think enables a happy, well-adjusted teenager to control his behavior? His conscience. If you want to prevent your child from developing a normal responsive conscience which will enable him to *control himself,* build your relationship with him on a punitive basis. Control his behavior primarily by spanking and scolding, especially spanking.

Another tragic consequence of corporal punishment is called *identification with the aggressor.* It is also a guilt-escaping mechanism. A child identifies (sides with) the punishing parent, coming to the place where he feels being aggressive and punitive is right. Then, of course, this child grows up, has children, and treats them as he himself was treated. This is why abusing parents were themselves usually ill-treated by their parents. This use of corporal punishment (or the threat of it) as the main way of handling a child is passed on from generation to generation. This in itself is bad enough. With the frightening advent of violence in all modes of mass communication, especially television, is it any wonder child abuse and all other forms of violence have become a national disgrace? Until we parents begin to proclaim the indispensable needs of a child, namely, unconditional love and loving discipline, the situation will continue to become worse. We parents must stand up against the avalanche of demanding critics who insist that beating a child (confusing punishment with discipline) should be the primary way of relating to him. Are you aware that some of the critics do not have children themselves? Until we give a child what he desperately needs, he (and we) will suffer.

I challenge you, dear parents, to look at every statistic regarding children and adolescents in our nation today—academics, attitudes, respect for authority, emotional disturbance, motivation, drugs, crime, and so on. The situation is horrible. I maintain that the principle reason for our national dilemma with youth today is that our children do not feel genuinely loved, accepted, and cared for. With the deafening roar of disciplinarians (actually punishment-oriented) on one side and advocates of vague, difficult-to-follow programs on the other, parents are confused.

Using designed programs such as those based on behavior modification techniques as the *primary* way of relating to your child is also a mistake. Like punishment, these programs do have a place in child rearing and can be very helpful, *but not as the principal way of relating to a child*. Some of these programs are quite good, but usually their techniques are used in place of unconditional love and loving discipline (training). Here is the error. These designed techniques can be of great value in certain situations (which we will mention later), but we parents must first make sure that our child's emotional tank is as full as possible before we resort to punishment or designed techniques. In most cases, if a child receives his required amount of unconditional love and loving discipline, the parents seldom need to resort to punishment or programs. Yes, punishment and techniques are at times necessary, quite helpful, and often good, but let's face it, they are not the best; appropriate love and guidance are.

We want the most positive, pleasant, loving relationship we can possibly have with a child. At the same time, we want him to develop self-control and act appropriately to the extent that he is able (considering his age, development, etc.). In order to see these two priceless happenings come to pass, parents must give their child two things. First, give him unconditional love, and give it appropriately. Second, give him loving discipline, that is, training in the most positive way possible. Training by all available means, in such a way that enhances a child's self-esteem and does not demean him or hurt his self-concept. Positive guidance to good behavior is far superior to negative punishment for poor behavior.

But no matter how well we do our jobs as parents, a child will sometimes misbehave. This is inevitable. There are no perfect parents and there is no perfect child.

So how should we handle misbehavior from a child? We will consider this in the next chapter.

9

Loving Discipline

Up to this point we have explored how to convey unconditional love to a child by proper use of eye contact, physical contact, focused attention, and discipline (training). We have found how important it is to make sure we keep a child's emotional tank full for only then can he develop to be his best. Only then can he develop full self-control and self-discipline. We found in chapter 8 that guidance toward right action is better than punishment for wrong action. Then we ended that chapter with the fact that every child will misbehave at times. Let's now consider how to deal with misbehavior.

In order to understand how to deal with a child's behavior, we must understand the irrational way in which all children think. This crucial area must be carefully considered. All children need and want love. They know they need love and they know they want it but the way in which they seek it is immature and irrational.

First, let's look at a rational way to obtain love. Say a man named Jim loved a woman named Carla. How would Jim be likely to win Carla's love? Acting immaturely, putting his worst foot forward, whining, pouting, being argumentative and demanding? Of course not. If Jim were mature, he would be at his best. He would put his best foot forward, remain calm, pleasant, helpful, kind, and considerate. When he was not sure of Carla's love, he would not resort to immature behavior; rather he would try to earn Carla's love. He would try to deserve it in her eyes. That's a rational way to obtain love.

But that is not the way a child does it, folks. The younger a child, the less mature he is. That makes sense, doesn't it? And the less mature he is, the more irrational he is. A child knows by nature how desperately he needs love. But he does not by nature try to deserve it or win it. This logic is beyond his inherent understanding. Eventually he may (or may not) learn this but he is not born with this capability.

What does a child do then, especially a younger child? A child communicates primarily with his behavior. He continually asks the question, "Do you love me?" How we answer that question determines many things. It determines a child's self-esteem, attitudes, feelings, peer relationships, and on and on. If his emotional tank is full, you can see it in his behavior. If it is empty, it is manifested by his behavior. Put it this way. Most behavior in a child is determined by how much he feels loved.

This is the irrationality of a child. Instead of winning our love and affection by good behavior, a child by nature continually *tests* our love by his behavior. "Do you love me?" If we answer that all-important question, "Yes, we love you," great! The pressure to seek love is then off a child and his behavior can be more easily controlled. If a child does not feel loved, by nature he is compelled more earnestly to ask, "Do you love me?" through his behavior. We may not like this behavior because there are only a limited number of ways a child may act, and many of these ways may be inappropriate for the occasion. It stands to reason that when anyone is desperate enough, his behavior may become inappropriate. Nothing makes a child more desperate than the lack of love.

This is the primary cause of misbehavior in a child. When his emotional tank is empty, he cries out behaviorally, "Do you love me?"

Is it fair then, or wise, to demand good behavior from a child without first making sure he feels loved? Without first filling his emotional tank?

What Does this Child Need?

Let me give you an example. My 16-year-old daughter Carey went to camp last summer. My nine-year-old boy was then the oldest child at home, and he liked it. He acted more maturely, and sought more responsibility. David liked being the oldest. It was great.

The problem was that eventually Carey had to come home. Well, on the day she returned, David's behavior regressed. He suddenly became whiny, discontented, pouty, somewhat angry, moody, and withdrawn.

What happened? Why the sudden, drastic change in David? What should I do as a parent? Punish David for his poor behavior? Send Carey back to camp? Tell David his five-year-old brother acts better than he? What would you do?

Well, let me explain what I did and why. Of course Carey's coming home and again becoming the oldest kid was hard on David. That's difficult for a seven-year-old (he was seven then) to handle. His behavior was the pleading question, "Do you love me? Do you love me now that Carey is home and I'm not the oldest any more? How does your love for me compare to your love for Carey? Is she more important? Can she take away your love from me?" Oh, the heartache for children at these times!

If I punished him at that time, how would David think I was answering his question, "Do you love me?" As soon as I could, I took David off to himself, held him close, and we talked for some time. Occasionally I told him in boy ways how much I loved him. I gave him eye and physical contact. As his emotional tank was filled, his mood changed back to his happy, outgoing self. It took about 15 to 20 minutes before he was off to play. David was happy and his behavior was fine. That was one of those special moments we talked about before. I think he will never forget that precious time together. I won't.

Please don't get the idea I'm a perfect father. I'm not. I've made many mistakes. But here was one situation I think I handled all right.

All this leads us to the realization that when our child misbehaves we must ask ourselves, "What does this child need?"

The tendency is for parents to ask, "What can I do to correct this child's behavior?" Unfortunately this question usually leads initially to punishment. It is then difficult to consider the real needs of a child and we may end up spanking him or sending him to his room. A child will not feel loved if we approach the handling of his misbehavior this way.

We should always begin by asking ourselves, "What does this child need?" Then we can proceed *logically* from there. Only then can we take care of the misbehavior, give him what he needs, *and* permit him to feel genuinely loved.

The next step is to ask ourselves, "Does the child need eye contact? Does he need physical contact? Does he need focused attention?" In short, does his emotional tank need filling? We parents must make sure that if the misbehavior is in any way caused by a need for any of these, we must first meet these needs. We as parents should not continue to correct a child's behavior until we have met his emotional needs.

This reminds me of a recent situation with our five-year-old son. I had been out of town for a few days and had returned home. Our five-year-old Dale was acting in a way which irritated me (and everyone else). He was doing all sorts of antics designed to aggravate the rest of the family, especially his nine-year-old brother. You see, Dale knows exactly what to do or say to make David climb the wall. And of course David can do the same to Dale. In fact, one son annoying the other is one of the first clues my dear wife and I have that an emotional tank needs filling.

Anyway, on this certain day, Dale was especially aggravating. He would needle his brother, pout, and make unreasonable demands. My first reaction, of course, was to really get on to him. Perhaps send him to his room; perhaps put him to bed; perhaps spank him. Then I stopped to think. "What does he need?" The answer came in an instant. I had been out of town. He had not seen me in three days and I had not really paid him much attention (no focused attention). No wonder the child was asking the old question, "Do you love me?" Actually Dale was asking, "Do you still love me after being gone so long and acting as though it didn't affect me?" Suddenly his behavior made sense. He desperately needed his daddy and his daddy was not giving him what he needed. If I had done anything other than give him what he needed, me, his behavior would have become worse. (Yes, even if I had spanked him.) He would have been deeply hurt, resentful, and I would have lost the opportunity to give him one of those special moments.

I can't tell you how thankful I am that I didn't goof on that one. I took Dale to our bedroom, held him close and said nothing. That normally active fellow was so still and quiet against me. He just sat there and absorbed that intangible nurturing. Gradually, as his emotional tank was filled, he came to life. He began talking in his confident, easygoing, spontaneously happy way. After a short conversation about my trip, he jumped down, and ran off. Where? To find his brother, of course. When I walked to the family room, they were playing contentedly together.

So we can see how vital it is always to be asking ourselves, "What does this child need?" If we do not, we will most assuredly skip prematurely into handling misbehavior inappropriately. We will miss chances to have those extremely important special moments with him. And we will punish a child at times which will hurt him in such a way that will create anger and resentment.

Fellow parents, if you miss this, you've wasted your time reading this book. Misbehavior should not be condoned but if it is dealt with in an inappropriate way, that is, too harshly or too permissively, we're going to have problems with that child. Yes, we must check misbehavior. We *must* not tolerate misconduct. But the first step is *not* punishment. Punishment is occasionally necessary but because of its negative effects from overuse, punishment should be used *only as a last resort*. It is far, far better to handle misbehavior positively, especially with genuine love and affection, than to punish a child, especially with corporal punishment. So the first step in any situation is to make sure a child's emotional needs are met. *His emotional tank must be full before caring parents can take any other action.*

Is There a Physical Problem?

The next question to ask ourselves in the face of misbehavior is, "Does a physical problem exist which is precipitating this behavior?" The younger a child, the more behavior is affected by physical needs. Is my child hungry? Is he tired, fatigued? Is he ill? Is he coming down with something, like a cold or flu? Is he in some kind of pain or other discomfort?

This does not mean misbehavior should be condoned if such a physical reason exists. (Misbehavior, in my opinion, should *never* be condoned.) It means that we parents must make sure we are taking care of what is *causing* the misbehavior as well as the misbehavior itself. It is certainly better to correct the misbehavior by giving a child what he needs—eye contact, physical contact, focused attention, water, food, a nap, relief of pain, or treatment of an illness—rather than punishment. Punishment may be appropriate but we must make sure that a child has all his physical and emotional needs met first.

How can we tell when punishment is appropriate and when it will be destructive? Excellent question. It brings us to the next step in our logical way of handling misbehavior.

Learn to Forgive

In my experience, the most destructive time to punish a child for misbehavior is when a child feels genuinely sorry for what he has done. The key word here is genuinely. If a child is genuinely remorseful for a wrong act, punishment (especially corporal punishment) would be harmful. The harm could come about principally in two ways.

First, if a child is already sorrowful for his inappropriate act, his conscience is alive and well. That's what you want! He has learned from his mistake. A good, healthy conscience is the best deterrent to repeating misbehavior. Punishment, especially corporal punishment, would remove the feelings of guilt and remorse and enhance the possibility for a child to forget the discomfort of these feelings and to repeat the misconduct.

Secondly, punishing a child under these circumstances could produce feelings of anger. When a child already feels genuinely contrite and remorseful for his act, his conscience is dealing severely with him. He is punishing himself. He needs and is seeking comfort and reassurance that, even though his deed was bad, he is a good child. He desperately needs this assurance at such a time. So if you make the mistake of spanking him at a time when he painfully needs affection, he is deeply hurt. Under such circumstances a child will then feel that he is bad as a person and that you, the parents, believe this to be true. The result is feelings of anger, hurt, resentment, and frequently bitterness that a child will carry with him indefinitely.

What should we parents do when a child commits a wrongful act and is genuinely sorry and remorseful about it? Scripture is a real help at this point. When we do wrong and are sorry for our wrongdoing, what does our heavenly Father do? He forgives us. Look at this writing of the psalmist: "Just as a father has compassion on his children, so the Lord has compassion on those who fear Him" (Ps. 103:13, NASB). With the tenderness, compassion and forgiveness that our heavenly Father gives to us under these circumstances, how can we then turn right around and punish *our* children?

The Apostle Paul warned of this mistake when he wrote, "Fathers, do not exasperate your children; instead, bring them up in the training and instruction of the Lord" (Eph. 6:4, NIV). I personally know of no surer way to provoke a child to anger, resentment, and bitterness than to punish him, especially physically, when he is genuinely sorry for his behavior. At these times we must learn to forgive.

Another reason it is essential to forgive a child under these circumstances is that he must learn how to feel forgiven during childhood or he will have problems handling guilt. Consider how many people are guilt-laden today (including Christians) because they have never learned to feel forgiven. These poor persons may actually be truly forgiven by God and others. But they still *feel* the guilt even though they know that they are forgiven. We can save a child untold problems with guilt if we will teach him how to deal with it, namely, by the feeling of forgiveness. And we can do this by forgiving him when he is genuinely sorry for a misconduct.

A Broken Window

I remember an experience I had in this regard, but again please remember, just because I am picking out an example of a time when I did something right as a father doesn't mean I'm a perfect father. It just means that there are advantages to being a writer. I can pick out an example to illustrate a point.

Recently I came home after a long, difficult day in which several things went wrong. I was exhausted and certainly not feeling my best. As soon as I got out of the car, my nine-year-old son ran to me. Usually David has a great big smile on his face and jumps up to give me a big bear hug. This time he was different. His face was so long and forlorn. He looked at me so sadly through his beautiful blue eyes, and said, "Dad, I have to tell you something."

Because of my state of mind, I didn't feel I could handle a big problem very well right then. So I said, "Let's talk about it later, OK, David?"

David looked at me very intently and replied, "Can't we talk about it now, Dad?"

Just then I reached to open the back door and noticed that one of the windows was broken. Somehow I figured out what was on David's mind.

Because I was in an irritable state of mind, I decided I had surely better handle this matter after I had relaxed. But David had followed me to my bedroom and pleaded, "Please let us talk about it now, Dad."

With that pleading look on his face, what could I say? I said, "OK, David what would you like to talk about?" (As if I didn't know.)

David told me how he and his friends were playing baseball close to the house and how a foul ball had hit a window and broken it. He knew he had done wrong and was obviously sorry about it. He was, through his behavior, asking, "Do you love me after what I did?"

So I took the boy on my lap and held him close to me for a little while, and said, "That's OK, David. That was an easy thing to do, and we can get the window fixed. Just play farther from the house, OK?"

That was a special moment. David was immediately filled with relief. He cried briefly and just rested in my arms for a few moments. I could just feel the love flow from this child's heart. One of the most wonderful moments of my life. Then David was his old happy, radiant self. He jumped up and was off.

I've learned so much from this type of experience. This was one of those opportunities that do not come every day. A child does not always feel genuinely sorry for his misconduct, so we must be constantly looking for this type of opportunity to actually do what we say we should do. At these times we are able to convey to a child that although we do not like his misconduct, we do love him no matter what. We love him unconditionally.

When a child is forgiven a misconduct, this does not mean he should not assume responsibility for its consequences. Restitution may be indicated. In the case of David's breaking the window, it may have been constructive to have him pay for the broken glass in an appropriate way, like working it off. But again, we must make sure that the restitution is in line with the child's age, level of development, and ability to handle it.

We mustn't be manipulated. I am sure you have heard a child say, "I'm sorry," when he wasn't. Quite frequently a child says, "I'm sorry" whenever he thinks he may be punished. Of course this is not being genuinely sorry or remorseful and we must be able to distinguish the difference.

Fortunately, it is seldom difficult to tell if a child is really sorry or not. The most obvious indication of a child's being manipulative in this way is his repeating the misbehavior. If David continued to play baseball near the house after the incident, I could conclude that I had been manipulated and other measures should be taken.

If a child frequently attempts to manipulate his parents in this manner, I would be quite concerned. It could be indicative that a child's sense of right and wrong are developing in a twisted way. He could be learning to use untruthful statements to gain an advantage, saying, "I'm sorry" simply to escape punishment. This particular behavior is a good example of what placing the cart before the horse will develop. When parents relate to a child primarily by using punishment to control behavior instead of first meeting a child's emotional needs, a child will develop all sorts of gimmicks to escape punishment. One of these is "I'm sorry" when the parents become angry or upset over a child's behavior.

This is a dangerous situation. A child is then learning to be insincere, dishonest, calculating, manipulative, and insensitive. There is one commodity which cuts straight across this mistake and reverses the trend. It is unconditional love.

In such a situation parents' good judgment is imperative. Parents are in the best position to discern whether a child is being truthful and sincere. If a child is frequently manipulative and untruthful, trouble is ahead and help should be sought.

However, any child can do this occasionally, just as any child occasionally will feel real sorrow and guilt for misbehavior. Wise, careful parents will realize there is a difference, discern the difference, and handle each situation appropriately.

In short, forgive a child when he is genuinely sorry, remorseful, and repentant for a misconduct. These infrequent opportunities are priceless ones and let him know beyond a doubt that you understand him, are genuinely concerned about him, and deeply love him regardless of anything else. This is unconditional love.

10

Discipline
—Requests, Commands, Rewards,
and Punishment

What we have considered thus far are by far the most important and crucial aspects of child rearing. If these principles are applied properly, most problems of raising a child will be alleviated or averted. Meeting a child's emotional needs and applying loving discipline will permit a healthy, strong, positive love-bond between parents and their child. When any problem with a child occurs, parents must reexamine the child's needs and fill them before doing anything else.

Please remember the material in the preceding chapters because, quite frankly, I am going into the part of discipline which I hate to put into print. Why? Because there are many parents who read a book such as this to glean from it only the material which they need to justify preconceived notions about child rearing. I am afraid parents will apply only this section of the book and completely miss the fact that punishment should be used only as a last resort.

I hope you are not such parents. I hope you will apply the first nine chapters before applying this one. Please love your child unconditionally and give him a superabundance of eye contact, physical contact, and focused attention. Please be careful not to love your child with possessiveness, seductiveness, vicariousness, or role-reversal. Please discipline (train) your child in *positive* ways such as guidance, example, modeling, and instruction. When your child misbehaves, ask yourself if he needs eye contact, physical contact, focused attention, rest, or water, and fill these needs first. When your child is sorry, remorseful, and repentant for a misbehavior, please forgive him, and let him know he is forgiven.

Fellow parents, if you are diligently doing these things, and other factors such as marriage are satisfactory, things should be going fairly well with your child. Your child should be happy, responsive, well-behaved, doing what you ask him to do (according to his age and level of development) without too much difficulty. I'm not saying everything should be *perfect,* but you should be satisfied with your child, your relationship with him, and the way he is progressing.

I am saying all this now because it is a tragic mistake to expect punishment *in itself* to provide anything but negative results. Punishment without a firm foundation of unconditional love and loving discipline (training) cannot but create a poor relationship between parents and their child. Unfortunately this is a common type of child rearing today. This is one reason children are generally having unprecedented problems today in every area, from academics to personality problems.

Requests

Proper behavior from a child is required first by requesting it. This is the most positive way of achieving good behavior. More importantly, requests instill a sense of personal responsibility in a child. A child feels that proper behavior is just as much his responsibility to do as it is his parents' responsibility to see that it is done. A child knows by nature that he has a choice in how to act. When parents *request* good behavior, a child knows his parents understand that he has ability to think and make decisions himself, has control over his behavior, and must learn to take responsibility for it. When requests instead of commands are used as much as possible, a child will consider his parents in alliance with him in helping him to mold his own behavior. This is so important.

If commands are primarily used in requiring proper behavior, a child may be obedient and well behaved. But his tendency will be to act properly only because Mommy or Daddy say so, not because proper behavior is best for him. He will not see his parents in alliance with him primarily for his own best interests. He will see them as requiring proper behavior for the sake of good order, quietness, and their own social acceptance, in fact, for their own interests.

It is crucial to understand that making requests is a very effective way of giving instructions. It does not make us permissive or less firm. Using requests is simply a more thoughtful, pleasant, considerate way of giving instructions to a child. This is especially true when you want your child to enjoy doing things without resenting it.

For example, once when I was taking a bath, I noticed there were no towels in the bathroom. My five-year-old son was passing by so I took advantage of the opportunity and said, "Dale, would you go down and get your daddy a towel, please?" Dale was very happy to do so and was back with a towel before I could say "Jack Robertson."

Another example. The teacher of my nine-year-old son's Sunday School class was having problems with rowdiness from the boys. I had a choice of being very authoritarian and demanding that David "behave himself," or talking over the problem with him, clarifying the issues, and then requesting his cooperation. I chose the latter, and ended the conversation with, "I want you to pay attention to the teacher, join in the discussions, and learn all you can. Will you do that, David?" So far so good.

Direct Instruction

The fact must be faced, however, that requests will not always suffice. Occasionally parents must be more forceful and give directions not by requests but by direct instruction (commands). This usually happens when a request is given to a child and he fails to carry it out. Before parents do anything else they must make sure that their request was appropriate, that it was suitable to the child's age, understanding, and ability to carry out. The most frequent mistake in this regard is asking a child to do something which seems to be within his ability and actually is not.

A classic example of this is asking a four-year-old child to pick up his things by himself. Unless there are only two or three things to pick up, this request is unreasonable. A parent must do the task *with* his child. Frequently a parent mistakenly will believe a task such as this is appropriate, gets angry when his child refuses or fails, and punishes him instead of helping him to accomplish the task.

Another real value in using requests whenever possible is to help you determine when a task is reasonable or not. You know your child better than anyone else. If on countless previous occasions your child would very willingly do a task when requested, but on one occasion he suddenly refuses, it is harmful to get angry and punish him. Obviously, because he has had no problems with this request in the past, *there is something wrong now.* Don't you want to know what it is? I surely would. I would do my best to find the problem, because it might be extremely important. I would certainly rather take care of the problem and see my child proceed to do the task willingly than force him to do it before understanding the situation. If the reason for my child's behavior was legitimate, then I would be the one who should be punished for forcing him to perform the task.

As a parent I have the responsibility and authority to see that my child behaves properly, but I am also responsible for my child's total welfare. I am responsible for seeing that my child is not hurt by misuse of my power and authority over him. His future happiness and welfare are heavily dependent on how I use my parental authority over him.

At this point I would like to insert a very important piece of advice and warning. The more parents use such authoritative techniques as commands, scolding, nagging, or screaming, the less effective they become. It is like the boy who yelled, "Wolf,

wolf!" so many times that it lost its effect. If parents normally use pleasant requests, the occasional use of direct commands, will be quite effective. The more parents use authoritative ways of telling a child what to do, the less response they will have. This is especially true if they are also angry, hostile, or hysterical when they do it.

For example, have you been in a home where the tension level is high? In these homes the parents have used essentially all their authority and reserve force just to discipline (train) their children in routine, daily events. When real forcefulness and authority are needed for unusual and really important situations, these poor parents have nothing in reserve to handle the situations. Their children then react as they usually do to their parents' wishes. They are no more responsive to emergency situations, for example, than to such mundane matters as tying a shoestring.

Parents, we must save the big salvos for the important situations. We must have reserve ammunition to handle critical situations. It is important to maintain pleasantness with a child by considerate, reasonable requests as much of the time as possible.

Recently I made the mistake of using a forceful order when a simple request would have sufficed. The two boys and I were home and I wanted to have the house clean before Pat came home from a weekend conference. I started out pretty well. I asked the boys to start cleaning up their bedroom while I made the beds. When I returned in a few minutes, they were busy doing their chore. But I noticed that they had thrown some clothes on the floor of their closet instead of hanging them up. David and Dale are usually obedient, easy-to-handle boys and a short word of explanation and simple request would have sufficed. But I was somewhat annoyed and I overreacted. I barked out some orders to hang up these clothes which they were "ruining." See the error I made? I should not have used such forcefulness when a simple explanation and request would have been sufficient.

I should have saved forcefulness for a time when I would really need a rapid response under difficult circumstances. For example, one Sunday after we parked in our church's parking lot,

Dale was walking around the car when another car pulled out. It was a dangerous situation. I yelled at Dale to run to me. Thank goodness he understood the urgency in my voice and responded immediately. If it had been my habit to yell at Dale, I know he would have responded routinely.

Another example occurred when my nine-year-old David and I were playing basketball with several friends. We all got carried away because we were having so much fun and we played much too long. Consequently we were all extremely tired. Then David fell when someone ran into him. He hurt his ankle slightly but this pain in a very fatigued young boy was more than he could handle at that particular moment. He became angry at the person who knocked him over and began telling him about it. I saw this as inappropriate behavior on David's part but also as a good learning experience for him.

First I was convinced that David's emotional tank was full. He had had much affection, eye contact, physical contact and focused attention that weekend. Secondly, I made a request. I asked David to go with me to a place where I could talk to him. He was too angry to respond. That is where I needed enough force to control him. The next level of use of force is to give direct instruction (command). I said, "David, come with me," in a firm tone. He immediately responded. When we were alone, and as he calmed down, we talked about getting so angry we lose control of our behavior, and how to prevent it. It was a very profitable time for David because he learned much about self-control over inappropriate anger.

Suppose David simply would not have responded as I wanted him to do and could not calm down or gain control over his anger even after I commanded him to do so. The next step would have been to take him to a place where he could be by himself. If I could not get him to do this by verbal instruction, then I would have had to go to the next level of forcefulness, the use of physical force. But even here I would use the least harsh method. I would take him by the hand, perhaps have one arm around his shoulder, and lead him to a quiet place. The point is to control a child's behavior in the most gentle, most considerate, and most loving way possible.

Defiance

It is entirely possible that David could have remained unresponsive to any verbal approach. He could have refused to do as I wanted him to do in that situation. It could have developed into a battle of the wills. This could then be called *defiance*.

Defiance is one of the few indications for punishment. Defiance is openly resisting and challenging authority—parental authority. It is stubbornly refusing to obey. Of course defiance, as well as any misbehavior, cannot be permitted. At these times, punishment is often indicated, and such times occasionally occur no matter what we do. However, parents must attempt to avoid such unpleasant encounters. Not by catering to a child's unreasonable whims or wishes, but by constantly reexamining their own expectations of their child, making sure their expectations are reasonable, considerate, and are in accordance with their child's age, level of development, and ability to respond. Yes, times which require punishment will come, but if parents find themselves punishing their child frequently, they had better reexamine their relationship with that child and what they expect from him.

Imagine that a child becomes obviously defiant and his defiant behavior does not respond to filling his emotional tank. He does not respond to requests nor to firm instruction (command), and he remains defiant. (Again, let me say this situation should be quite rare. When it occurs, make sure you have tried everything before considering punishment.) He must be punished, but how?

Appropriate Punishment

Determining the appropriate punishment is seldom easy. The punishment must fit the offense. A child is sensitively aware of fairness and consistency. He knows when parents have overreacted or have been too harsh with him. He also knows when parents are too accepting of poor behavior. He detects inconsistency either with him alone or in comparison with other children, especially siblings. This is the reason parents must be firm with their child, always demanding appropriate behavior and not being afraid to continually love and discipline (train) him simultaneously. Parents must remain flexible, especially regarding punishment.

Flexibility is necessary for several reasons. First, parents make mistakes. If you feel parents should not make changes in their disciplinary actions once a decision is made, you are going to back yourself into a corner. *Of course* parents can change their minds, and lessen or increase the punishment. (Remember that this is a disadvantage to corporal punishment, for once done, it can't be changed.)

Naturally, parents don't want to change their minds so often that they are wishy-washy and confuse the child. I mean, for instance, if a punishment is set forth, say confinement to the bedroom for one hour, and later parents discover extenuating facts which show this punishment to be too harsh, it is logical and proper to explain this to the child and lessen the punishment. If the child has already been punished or for some other reason has suffered inappropriate punishment, it is perfectly all right for parents to apologize to the child and attempt to make the situation right.

Parents must be flexible in order to change their approach to their child when indicated. Parents must also be flexible to be able to apologize. The need to occasionally change decisions and the need to apologize occurs in every home.

Being flexible in order to appropriately change our approach to handling discipline (training) and being firm are two different things. Both are essential. Firmness first of all includes what our expectations are regarding a child and his response to requests. If our expectations are too rigid (for example, expecting a two-year-old to consistently respond to first requests) we are being unreasonable. A normal two-year-old will naturally be negative most of the time and seem to be quite disobedient and defiant. But this is a normal stage of development, let's call it "two-year-old negativism." Punishment for this is unwarranted. Loving parents of a two-year-old will, of course, be firm, but firm in *limit setting,* not in punishment. These parents will control the child's behavior by gently maneuvering the child physically, for example, picking him up, turning him around, guiding him, or placing him in the correct place or position.

This "two-year-old negativism" is crucial for normal child development. This is one of the ways each of us had to separate ourselves psychologically from our parents. It may appear to be defiance but it is distinctively different. One difference between two-year-old negativism and defiance is belligerence. Two-year-old negativism is normal and should not be punished. Belligerent defiance on the other hand cannot be tolerated and must be dealt with.

As a child becomes older, his ability to respond to verbal requests increases and by the time he reaches four and one-half (this varies from child to child), parents can expect him to respond to first requests. I fully expect my children to respond to first requests. If they do not, they know that action will be taken. Of course they are free to make an appropriate statement regarding the request, if they have any question about it. But unless I change the request, they know they must carry it out.

It is so important to remember that being firm does not mean being unpleasant. We must be firm in our expectations and enforcement of these expectations, but we will be just as effective by doing it pleasantly. Loving firmness does not require us to be angry, loud, authoritative, or otherwise unpleasant.

One of the most important lessons in child rearing is that every child needs to experience all the ways of loving simultaneously. He needs eye contact, physical contact, focused attention, *and* discipline *simultaneously.* A child must have our love and firmness together. None of these things are mutually exclusive. Being firm does not negate affection. Being affectionate does not lessen firmness or foster permissiveness. *Lack of firmness and limit setting fosters permissiveness but love and affection do not.*

When parents have conscientiously provided all the preceding means of loving and disciplining a child, and he remains belligerently defiant, the parents must punish him. This type of defiance must be broken. The punishment must be severe enough to break the belligerent defiance, but it must also be as mild as possible to prevent the problems we have already discussed. If a command or explanation to a child is sufficient to break the defiance, why be more punitive? If sending a child to his room for a period is required and will suffice, fine. If taking a privilege away from a child is necessary to crush the defiance, proceed to do so. Let's face it, corporal punishment is sometimes necessary to break a pronounced belligerent defiance, but only as a last resort.

Be Careful

When corporal punishment is used, we must be careful in several respects. First, the child must understand exactly why he is being punished. Explain to him in terms of his behavior exactly what he has done wrong. Words such as "bad boy" can hurt the child's self-esteem and should not be used.

Secondly, parents must be careful not to inflict any physical damage on the child. For example, it is easy to hurt a finger inadvertently.

Thirdly, immediately after the punishment, as the child is crying, he should be left alone. Parents should stay nearby, however, listening for the crying to stop. When a child's crying has subsided and he is looking around, a child is again asking, "Do you love me? Do you still love me?" Parents should then give the child an abundance of eye contact, physical contact, and focused attention to reassure him that he is indeed loved.

Behavior Modification

Finally, I think it appropriate to mention *behavior modification*. This is a system of thought which is in wide use today concerning the handling of children. Very basically, behavior modification utilizes positive reinforcement (interjecting a positive commodity into a child's environment), negative reinforcement (withdrawing a positive commodity from a child's environment), and punishment (interjecting a negative commodity into a child's environment). An example of positive reinforcement is rewarding a child for an appropriate behavior by giving him a piece of candy or fruit. An example of negative reinforcement is withdrawing television privileges from a child for inappropriate behavior. An example of punishment (sometimes called aversive technique) is pinching him on the trapezius muscle for inappropriate behavior.

It is beyond the scope of this book to speak to this subject in depth. However, a few important points should be made.

First of all, such emphasis has been made concerning behavior modification that such techniques are frequently substituted for emotional nurturing. If behavior modification is overused by parents in relating to a child, a child will not feel loved. Why? First of all, the very foundation of behavior modification is *conditional*. A child receives a reward only if he *behaves* a certain way. Secondly, behavior modification is not concerned with feelings or the emotional needs of a child (love). Consequently parents, using behavior modification as the primary way of relating to a child, cannot convey unconditional love to that child.

For instance, consider the example I used in the last chapter regarding filling Dale's emotional tank when he misbehaved following my three-day absence. A strict behaviorist would say I was rewarding Dale for his misbehavior by giving him affection at that time. See the difference? Parents cannot *primarily* use behavior modification in relating to their child and love their child unconditionally.

Another problem with relating to a child primarily by behavior modification is that a child will derive an inappropriate value system. He will learn to do things primarily for a reward. A "what's in it for me?" orientation will develop. An example of this occurred at the home of a dear friend of ours. He happens to be a strict behaviorist and was raising his children as closely to the behavior modification concept as he could. One evening, when we were eating at their home, he said, "Jerry is just three and he can count to a hundred already. Watch this." He went up to his son and said, "Jerry, count to a hundred and I'll give you an M and M." Jerry instantly replied, "I don't want an M and M." If we want our child to do things for the satisfaction of doing them or for the pride of a job well done, we had best not overuse behavior modification. The end result is inappropriate motivation.

One last problem with the use of behavior modification is this. If parents overuse these techniques, a child will learn to gain what he wants by using the same method on the parents. He will behave as the parents wish *in order to get something he wants.* Most persons would call this manipulation. One of the surest ways of encouraging your child to become cunning and manipulative is to use behavior modification techniques too often.

Now that I've expounded on the negative aspects of behavior modification, let me express the positive. There is a place for these techniques in child rearing, but not as the primary way of relating to a child (the primary way must be unconditional love).

Behavior modification should be used for specific, recurring behavioral problems for which a child is neither sorry nor defiant. This type of problem must also be specific enough to be easily defined and understood by a child.

Let me give you an example of this type of problem which we encountered in our home. About six months ago, our two boys were at stages where they frequently fought with each other. Of course, neither one was remorseful about this. Forgiveness was certainly inappropriate. And neither one was defiant about it. Requests did not work. Commands had effect only for a few hours. Punishments also had brief effects and were quite unpleasant for everyone. You know what worked? You've probably guessed it, a reward system.

We used a chart-with-stars technique. One star for every 15 minutes of peace, gradually increasing the time interval until the fighting was extinguished. We gave each boy an appropriate reward for a certain number of stars. It worked beautifully and we had "peace in the valley."

However, one word of warning about this type of technique. It takes time, consistency, real effort, and persistence. Don't start something like this unless you are prepared to stick with it and be consistent. Otherwise it will fail.

There are numerous good books on behavior modification to tell you more about specific techniques.

This has been a long chapter but allow me to make one more point. As you can tell, good child rearing requires balance. A child needs everything we have discussed: eye contact, physical contact, focused attention, discipline, requests, firmness, flexibility, commands, forgiveness, punishment, behavior modification, instruction, guidance, example, and active listening. But we must give our child these things in *proper measure*. I hope our discussions help you to do this in a way that will enable your child to feel unconditionally loved.

11

Children with Special Problems

Why do children with special problems such as diabetes, learning disabilities, deafness, hyperactivity, or mental retardation generally have markedly greater emotional and behavioral problems? The answer to this question is extremely complex. To explain why children in each of these problem areas are more prone to emotional and behavioral disturbance is beyond the scope of this small book.

However, a few very pertinent points would be helpful to every parent of such a child. Some of these facts are closely related to conveying love to our children.

Perceptual Problems

First, let's look at the general area of perceptual problems. To perceive is difficult to define, but let's try. It can mean to grasp or take in information through the senses to the mind, in which case a child with perceptual problems has difficulty taking in information from his environment and transmitting it to his mind. Consequently when such information as visual images, sound, and touch is processed in a child's mind, he has difficulty understanding it clearly. His understanding of his environment is distorted in those areas where his misperceptions lie.

Using this very broad and simplified definition of perceptual problems, we can see that many special problems can be included. Visual problems, hearing problems, certain neurological diseases, and many types of learning disabilities have one thing in common: each child suffering from one of these disorders has a distorted conception of his surroundings. In one or more ways his incoming stimuli or information are distorted to him.

Do you see the great significance of this beyond the perceptual disability per se? Every way we have to convey our love to a child requires the use of one or more of the perceptual senses. Eye contact requires the perceiving of visual imagery. Physical contact requires the use of the sense of touch which in itself is overwhelmingly complex. Focused attention requires the use of all of our senses. So if there is enough perceptual distortion in any of these areas, a child's understanding of how we feel about him can be distorted. This makes it more difficult to convey our love to this particular child.

This difficulty in feeling loved is one big reason perceptually handicapped children generally have less than adequate self-concepts. It is one reason they usually become increasingly depressed as they grow older. This frequently results in rather severe emotional and behavioral disorders, especially in early adolescence.

The common story of a perceptually handicapped child with resultant learning disabilities is that this unfortunate child cannot keep up academically or in other ways with his peers. He makes poor grades or is in other ways forced to endure continual degrading experiences. Even in nongraded situations he realizes his deficiencies. As he goes into the pre and early adolescent years, he becomes increasingly depressed. Depression in this age group is unlike any other. Generally these children do not look or act depressed unless the depression has reached severe depths. Typically 12-, 13-, and 14-year-old adolescents manifest their depression by difficulty in paying attention in the classroom (decreased attention span and ability to concentrate) with a resultant dropping of grades. Subsequently, prolonged boredom sets in with decreased interest in wholesome activities. At this stage the youngster is profoundly miserable.

If the boredom continues, eventually the teenager will act out his depression and misery. A severely depressed and bored girl in this predicament may then become promiscuous, use drugs, run away, or may try other antisocial behaviors. A boy in a comparable situation will be prone to act out similarly but is usually more inclined to violent activities such as stealing and fighting.

If we know that perceptually handicapped children are almost predisposed to poor self-concept feelings of being unloved and unacceptable, and of depression, how can we help them? I firmly believe that the area where they require the greatest help is the area which is largely overlooked. You guessed it, these children need most of all to feel genuinely, unconditionally loved. They will then be better able to overcome their handicaps.

How do we do this? The same way we give our love to all children, except that we must remember that although their perceptions are distorted in some areas, they are seldom distorted in all sensual modalities. These children almost always need more affection and other means of conveying love in order to feel loved. In addition, these poor children need our love to be given to them in more direct, simplified, straightforward, and accentuated ways. We must also give it to them in a somewhat more intense manner. All this is necessary to assure that these children do not misunderstand our feeling toward them, that they get a *clear message* from our hearts to theirs. Our love-communications with such children must be clear and strong.

Other Medical Problems

Children with chronic (long standing) medical problems are also prone to emotional and behavioral problems. This is especially true of medical problems which require close supervision and continual attention such as juvenile diabetes. Taking care of young children with this disease requires tremendous time and effort by parents. So much so that it is difficult not to devote one's full attention to treating the disease and overlooking other needs of the children. This is exactly what happens concerning the emotional needs of most of these children. The caring parents become so intent, for example, on giving the right doses of insulin, regulating the diet, doing glucose determinations and the like, that these necessary procedures replace the natural giving of love. As worthwhile as they are, these medical duties are no substitute for unconditional love given through eye contact, physical contact, and focused attention. As children grow older, especially during adolescence, they become increasingly angry, resentful, and bitter about their disease. Because of the fore-mentioned substitution of medical care for love, the children resent the disease and their parents. They become hostile and defiant not only toward parental authority but all authority. They are inclined to depression and all of its consequences. Worst of all, they frequently use the seriousness of their illness to defy parents and express anger and frustration. This may be done by taking too much insulin, eating too many carbohydrates, and so on. Many actually kill themselves as an angry, defiant act.

Of course there are other reasons in this complex illness which contribute to young patients' bitter and destructive attitudes. In my experience, however, there are two principal reasons why these poor children become so intensely resentful and defiant. The first is as we just discussed, substitution of medical procedures as a manifestation of love. The other is poor limit-setting and lack of behavioral control by the parents. The parents may feel pity for the children in their illness. They may also feel guilt, fear, or depression. If the parents cannot control the children's behavior in the same manner as they would other children, namely, with firmness, the children will be able to manipulate the parents. This is especially easy for chronically ill children to do. They can use their illness to control their parents. By taking advantage of the parents' guilt and pity, by making the parents fearful that the children's condition may worsen, and even by using the outright threat of purposely succumbing to the illness.

These dynamics may occur to some extent with any children

with any prolonged disability, illness, or other problem. For example, asthma, chronic bronchitis, heart defects, physical deformity, mental retardation, seizure disorders, neurological diseases, muscular diseases, dental problems, and even learning disabilities. The list goes on and on.

So, dear parents, if your child has any handicap, a problem of any kind, do not become so wrapped up with the problem that you neglect the child. He needs your unconditional love far more than anything else. Far more than any medical care, no matter how necessary. Far more than braces, far more than tutoring or other academic remediation, far more than any exercise, and far more than any medicine. The most indispensable ingredients in your child's life are you and your giving unconditional love to him. With that, your child can derive the strength and will to overcome and develop.

The Resistant Child

I would like to consider help for the resistant child, namely, one who is resistant to receiving affection. Yes, believe it or not, many children are naturally (congenitally) resistant to the natural ways of giving affection and love. They resist eye contact, they do not want to be touched, and they do not care for focused attention.

This may occur in varying degrees. Some children are only mildly resistant while others are quite uncomfortable with the conveying of love. Some children may be comfortable with one way of conveying love but not another. Each child is unique.

The resistant child is invariably an enigma to his parents. Caring parents instinctively know that their child needs affection and other forms of emotional nurturing, but when they try to meet this need, the child finds innumerable ways to avoid receiving love. What a dilemma. Many parents eventually resign themselves to what they conclude is "what the child wants." They assume that the child does not need their attention, love, and affection. This is a disastrous mistake.

Even the extremely resistant child needs everything we have talked about concerning unconditional love. However, since he is uncomfortable accepting it, we parents must gradually teach this child to receive love comfortably.

We can begin by understanding the five periods during which a child is able to receive love. During these periods the child's defenses are down and he is able to relate closely enough on the emotional level to be receptive. Of course every child is different. One child may be more receptive during one period and less receptive during another. It behooves parents to know when their child is most receptive to love and affection.

The first receptive period I would like to mention is when a child finds something to be quite humorous. For instance, a child may be watching television and see a funny scene. At this time parents have the opportunity to make eye contact, physical contact, and focused attention while commenting on the humorous subject. Parents must usually be quick in doing this because the defenses of a truly resistant child are down only briefly. We've got to "get in and get out" or a child may defend against similar tactics in the future.

The second period of receptivity is when a child has accomplished something for which he is justifiably proud. It cannot be just anything. The accomplishment must be something a child feels genuinely good about. At these times, parents can make eye and physical contact (and focused attention if appropriate) while praising a child. Again, we must be careful not to overdo it, especially by prolonging it; "get in and get out."

The third receptive period is at such times when a child is not well physically. A child may be ill or hurt, and his receptivity at these times is somewhat unpredictable. Sometimes illness or pain may increase a child's ability to receive affection, but at other times a child's resistance may increase. We parents should continually monitor this in order to take advantage of opportunities to give love at these times of illness or pain. A child will never forget special moments such as these.

The fourth period of receptivity occurs when a child is hurt emotionally. This frequently happens when he has a conflict with peers and the peers have taken unfair advantage of him. At these times of emotional pain, many resistant children become able to accept our showing love to them.

The fifth receptive period largely depends upon previous experience of a particular child. For example, one child may have had many pleasant, meaningful experiences while going on long walks with his parents. Such a child will quite likely be more receptive to parental conveying of love while on walks. Another child may have had pleasant experiences at bedtime when his parents would read, pray, and talk with him. This child will naturally be inclined to be more receptive at bedtime. This is why providing routine times of pleasant, warm experiences for a child is very important and pays large dividends to child and parents. Bedtime routine, for example, is a good investment.

In a nutshell, all children need the natural ways of conveying love. Eye contact, physical contact, and focused attention. If a child is not receiving an ample amount, we had best find out why and correct the situation.

We have discussed only a few possible problems which can prevent a child from receiving what he so desperately needs. I wish we had the space and time to talk about other children with special problems, such as grieving children, children of divorce, depressed children, children with terminal illness, and teenagers.

12

Helping Your Child Spiritually

One of the chief complaints we hear from teenagers today is the failure of their parents to give them ethical or moral standards to live by. This yearning is expressed by older children in many ways. One adolescent says he needs a "meaning in life." Another wants a "standard to guide her." Other seeking youngsters long for "higher guidance," "something to hold on to," or "something to show me how to live."

These desperate cries do not come from a few unhappy, discontented teenagers. Most adolescents are feeling and expressing these yearnings. They are confused, terribly confused, in this existential area of living. It is quite unusual to find young people who have "got it together" in regard to a meaning and purpose in this life, who are at peace with themselves and their world, and who have perspective and understanding about living in this confused, changing, fearful world today.

A child first looks to his parents for direction in this area. Whether he finds what he needs from his parents depends on two things. The first is whether the parents have it themselves. The second is whether a child can identify with his parents in such a way as to incorporate and accept parental values. A child who does not feel loved will find this difficult.

The First Requirement

Let's look at the first requirement that is necessary in giving a child that longed for meaning to life. We parents must possess a foundation upon which to base our lives and which can withstand the test of time. Something that will support us through every phase of living: adolescence, young adulthood, middle age, old age, marriage crises, financial crises, children's crises, energy crises, and especially, a rapidly changing society in which spiritual values are swiftly eroding. We parents must have that crucial foundation upon which we base our lives in order to give it to our child. In my opinion, it is the most valuable treasure we can pass on to our offspring.

What is this indispensable possession which gives purpose and meaning to life and is transferable to our child? Many have sought after it since the beginning of civilization but few have really found it. Philosophers have been struggling with these questions and answers for centuries. International diplomats have occasionally claimed some answers. Government planners are claiming to have answers even now, and their diligently planned legislation will leave hearts just as empty and longing as before, but more dependent upon man's (government's) control. The field of mental health offers help concerning emotional problems, mental disturbances, psychophysiological disorders, adaptational problems, and marital disharmony.

But this treasurable, peace-giving possession which every heart craves is a Person. He is intimately personal, yet can be shared with another. He is strengthening in times of conflict, yet is comforting in times of distress. He gives wisdom in times of confusion, yet gives correction in times of error. He provides help in times past and present, yet promises even more in the future. He gives direction and guidance at all times, yet does not send us out alone—He stays closer than a brother.

He gives directions to be carried out, yet gives amazingly wonderful promises to those who are willing to obey. He allows loss and pain at times, but He always heals and replaces the loss with something better. He does not force Himself upon us, but patiently waits to be accepted. He does not coerce us into doing His will, but is deeply distressed and hurt when we follow the wrong path. He wants us to love Him because He first loved us, but He gave us a free will to choose Him or reject Him. He wants to take care of us, but refuses to force Himself upon us. His greatest desire is to be our Father, but He will not intrude. If we want what He wants, a loving, caring, Father-child relationship with Him—we must accept His offer. He is too considerate to force it. He is waiting for you and me to become His children. Of course, as you have guessed, He must be a personal God.

This personal, intimate relationship with God through His Son Jesus Christ is the most important thing in life. This is the "something" which our young people are yearning for: the "meaning in life," "something to count on," "higher guidance," "something to bring comfort when everything seems to be falling apart." It is all there.

Do you have it? If you do not, seek help from a minister or Christian friend, or write me through the publisher and I will send you helpful material.

The Second Requirement

The second requirement necessary in order to give a child what we have is that a child identify with his parents so as to accept and incorporate the parents' values.

As you recall, if a child does not feel loved and accepted, he has real difficulty identifying with his parents and their values. Without a strong, healthy love-bond with his parents, a child reacts to parental guidance with anger, resentment, and hostility. He views each parental request (or command) as an imposition and learns to resist it. In severe cases, a child learns to consider each parental request with such resentment that his total orientation to parental authority (and eventually to all authority, including God's) is doing the opposite of what is expected of him.

With this type of attitude and orientation, you can see how difficult it becomes to give your child your moral and ethical value system.

In order for a child to identify with his parents (relate closely with them) and be able to accept their standards, he must feel genuinely loved and accepted by them. To give a child the close relationship with God which they possess, parents must make sure that a child feels unconditionally loved. Why? Because this is the way God loves us—unconditionally. It is extremely difficult for persons who do not feel unconditionally loved by their parents to feel loved by God. This is the greatest and most common obstacle to many people in establishing a personal relationship with God. Parents must prevent this happening in their own children.

How do parents ensure that their child is prepared and ready to accept God's love? By ensuring that they fill his emotional needs and keep his emotional tank full. Parents cannot expect a child to find a close, warm, *rewarding* relationship with God unless they have cared for him emotionally and he has such a relationship with them.

Yes, I have seen children who were raised by the rod become Christians. But because they were raised primarily by punishment instead of unconditional love, these unfortunate people seldom have a healthy, loving, warm relationship with God. They tend to use their religion punitively against others under the guise of "helping" them. They use biblical commandments and other scriptural statements to justify their own harsh, unloving behavior. They also tend to set themselves up as spiritual magistrates dictating the propriety of others. It is possible, of course, for any child to eventually find his way into God's loving arms and to accept His love. With God anything is possible. Unfortunately, a child's chances are markedly diminished if his parents have not given him a loving foundation.

So there are two requirements essential to helping a child spiritually: A parent's personal relationship with God, and a child's assurance that he is unconditionally loved.

A Child's Memory
The next important thing to know about a child is how his

memory operates. Remember that a child is much more emotional than cognitive. He therefore remembers feelings much more readily than facts. A child can remember how he felt in a particular situation much easier than he can remember the details of what went on.

Let me give you a very pertinent example. A child in a Sunday School class will remember exactly how he felt long after he forgets what was said or taught.

So, in some ways, whether a child's experience was pleasant or unpleasant is much more important than the details of what a teacher taught. By pleasant, I do not mean that a teacher need cater to a child's desire for fun and frolic. I mean treating a child with respect, kindness, and concern. Make him feel good about himself. Do not criticize, humiliate, or otherwise put him down. Naturally, what a child is taught is extremely important, but if it is a degrading or boring experience for a child, he is very likely to reject even the very best teaching, especially if morality and ethics are involved. It is from this type of situation that a child develops a bias against religious matters, and tends to consider church people as hypocrites. This attitude is difficult to rectify and can continue with him for a lifetime. On the other hand, if the learning experience is a pleasant one, a child's memories of religious things will be pleasant and can then be incorporated into a child's own personality.

As an illustration, friends of ours have an eight-year-old son, Michael, who used to enjoy Sunday School and being taught about spiritual things. There was no problem getting him to go to the Lord's house. Sadly, one Sunday morning, Michael and another energetic boy were talking and laughing during a presentation by the teacher. Thoughtlessly, Michael and his friend were put in a small room by themselves and made to write, "Thou shalt honor thy mother and thy father," over and over until his parents came to get him. The unreasonableness and insensitiveness of that unjust and humiliating punishment had dramatic effects. It induced such anger, hurt, and resentment that Michael began holding animosity toward anything spiritual. He refused to return to his church and, of course, his conception of God was severely damaged. Only after several months have his loving parents been able to help Michael again trust spiritual truths. This type of thing, in greater or lesser extremes, happens when the importance of the teacher's teaching is placed before the emotional welfare of a child. Emotionality and spirituality are not entirely separate entities. One is quite related to and dependent upon the other. For this reason, if parents want to help a child spiritually, they must care for him first emotionally. Because a child remembers feelings much more easily than facts, there must be a series of pleasant memories upon which to accumulate the facts, especially spiritual facts.

A Popular Misconception

At this point, I would like to examine a popular misconception. It goes something like this: "I want my child to learn to make his own decisions after he is exposed to everything. He shouldn't feel he has to believe what I believe. I want him to learn about different religions and philosophies; then when he has grown up he can make his own decision."

This parent is copping out or else is grossly ignorant of the world we live in. A child brought up in this manner is indeed one to be pitied. Without continual guidance and clarification in ethical, moral, and spiritual matters, he will become increasingly confused about his world. There are reasonable answers to many of life's conflicts and seeming contradictions. One of the finest gifts parents can give to a child is a clear, basic understanding of the world and its confusing problems. Without this stable base of knowledge and understanding, is it any wonder many children cry to their parents, "Why didn't you give me a meaning for all this? What's it all about?"

Another reason this approach to spirituality is grossly negligent is this. More and more groups, organizations, and cults are offering destructive, enslaving, and false answers to life's questions. These people would like nothing more than to find a person who was brought up in this seemingly broad-minded way. He is easy prey for any group offering concrete answers, no matter how false or enslaving (remember the Moonies?).

It is amazing to me how some parents can spend thousands of dollars and go to any length of political manipulation to make sure their child is well prepared educationally. Yet, for the most important preparation of all, for life's spiritual battles and finding real meaning in life, a child is left to fend for himself and made easy prey to cultists.

Every Child Loves a Story

How do parents prepare their child spiritually? Organized religious instruction and activities are extremely important to a developing child. However, nothing influences a child more than his home and what he is exposed to there. This holds true regarding spiritual things as well. Parents must be actively involved in a child's spiritual growth. They cannot afford to leave it to others, even superb church youth workers.

First, parents themselves must teach their child spiritual concerns. They must teach him not only spiritual facts, but how to apply them in his everyday life. This is not easy.

It is quite simple to give a child basic scriptural facts such as who different Bible persons were and what they did. But that is not what we are ultimately after. What we want is for a child to understand what meaning biblical characters and principles have for him personally. We can only do this at somewhat of a sacrifice to ourselves, as with focused attention. Actually, what we are speaking of does include focused attention. We must be willing to spend time alone with a child in order to provide for his emotional needs as well as his spiritual. In fact whenever possible, why not do them simultaneously?

Bedtime is usually the best time to accomplish this, for most children are then eager to interact with their parents. Whether it is because their emotional tanks need filling or because they want to delay bedtime makes little difference. The point is that it is a great opportunity to meet the emotional needs of a child, give him spiritual training and guidance, and do it in an atmosphere which a child will remember fondly. By what other means can parents give so much to a child in such an economical way?

Every child loves a story. So I personally begin by reading a story of my child's choice. Sometimes it is a secular story. At other times it is a story from a Christian book. Sometimes my child wants me to make up a story about "Bing Bing and Boing Boing," "The Great Rootabaga," and other stories I've made up before.

Then I read a short devotional story from a children's Christian book. My boys love to answer questions about the stories so I prefer books that have questions after each story. The one we presently are using is *More Little Visits with God* by Allan Hart Jahsmann and Martin P. Simon (St. Louis: Concordia Publishing House, 1961).

If my nine-year-old David is particularly keyed up, I have found that more action-packed stories hold his interest better. For this reason I often use the six-volume version of *The Picture Bible for All Ages,* by Iva Hath and Andre Le Blanc (Elgin, Illinois: David C. Cook Publishing Co., 1973).

As a child answers the questions, there are always similarities and applications to what is going on in his own life. The hard part is getting the message across to a child and, because many parents feel awkward and inept at this, they usually give it up, especially if a child doesn't contribute much. Don't let these things stop you! Whether a child appears to be responding or not, you can rest assured that you are strongly influencing him. Your time spent with your child in this way will have far-reaching effects. If you don't influence your child in the area of the supernatural now, someone else will do it later.

Share Your Spiritual Life

I'd like to cover one more point about helping a child spiritually. With the factual knowledge gained from church, Sunday School, and home, a child only has the raw materials with which to grow in his spiritual life. He must learn to use this knowledge effectively and accurately to become a mature person spiritually. To do this a child must have the experience of walking with God daily and learning to rely on Him personally.

The best way to help a child with this is to share your own spiritual life with him. Of course, what you share with a child and how much you share again depends on the child, his age, level of development, and ability to comprehend and handle it.

As a child matures, we parents want to gradually increase sharing with him how we ourselves love God, walk daily with Him, rely on Him, seek His guidance and help, thank Him for his love, care, gifts, and answered prayer.

We want to share these things with our child *as they happen,* not afterward. Only in that way can a child get on-the-job training. Sharing past experiences is simply giving additional factual information, not letting a child learn for himself through his own experience. There is a lot of truth in the old statement, "Experience is the best teacher." Let him share in yours. The sooner a child learns to trust God, the stronger he will become.

A child needs to learn how God meets all personal and family needs, including financial. He needs to know what his parents are praying for. For example, he needs to know when you are praying for the needs of others. He should (again, as appropriate) know of problems for which you are asking God's help. And don't forget to keep him informed about how God is working in your life, how He is using you to minister to someone. And, of course, a child should certainly know you are praying for him and for his individual, particular needs.

Finally, a child must be taught by example how to forgive and how to find forgiveness both from God and people. Parents do this first of all by forgiving, as mentioned in chapter 9. Next, when they make a mistake which hurts a child, they admit the mistake, apologize, and ask his forgiveness. I cannot overstress how important this is. So many people today have problems with guilt. They cannot forgive and/or they cannot feel forgiven. What can be more miserable? But the fortunate person who has learned how to forgive those who offend him and is able to ask and receive forgiveness, demonstrates a mark of mental health.

Fellow parents, I hope you will seriously consider the contents of this book. It was written expressly for you by another parent whose strongest desire is to see his children and yours grow into strong, healthy, happy, and independent adults. I hope you will even read this small volume over and over. I for one must be continually reminded how to love my children.